What is Marxism?

AF552792

What is Marxism?

Rob Sewell
Mick Brooks
Alan Woods

What is Marxism?
Rob Sewell, Mick Brooks and Alan Woods

© Wellred Publications 2008
© Aakar Books for South Asia 2010

First Published in India, 2010
Reprinted 2018
Reprinted 2024

ISBN 978-93-5002-079-1 (Pb)

Published with the permission from Wellred Publications, London for publication and sale only in South Asia.

All rights reserved. No part of this book may be reproduced or transmitted, in any form or by any means, without prior permission of the publisher.

Published by
AAKAR BOOKS
28 E Pocket IV, Mayur Vihar Phase I
Delhi 110 091, India
www.aakarbooks.com

Printed at
D.K. Fine Art Press, Delhi

contents

Introduction

"Socialism, having become a science, demands the same treatment as any other science - *it must be studied.*" Frederick Engels

We are repeatedly told, like some old gramophone record stuck in a groove, that Marxism is either irrelevant, or out-dated, or even dead. Yet, if that were true, why are so many books and articles churned out year-on-year attacking Marxism? Clearly the powers that be are rattled or indeed frightened by these "dead" ideas. This is because Marxism is far from dead. Marxism is, in fact, becoming increasingly attractive in this epoch of instability, crisis, war and the ever-widening gulf between the classes. The old mole of revolution, to use Marx's phrase, is borrowing ever deeper into the foundations of society.

In typical fashion, a recent critic, Niall Ferguson, Professor of Political and Financial History at Oxford, vents his spleen on Marxism by attacking Marx as a "washout" and a "class traitor", for siding with the working class instead of the bourgeoisie. Our learned Professor goes on to brand Marx as the advocate of a "socialist utopia [which] turned out to be a corrupt tyranny", presumably a reference to Stalinism, which had nothing in common with Marx or his teachings. Consumed with spite, he then goes on to criticise Marx's *Capital* as "long, verbose, abstruse" and ranking as one of the most "unreadable books of all time".

Another bourgeois critic, Dominic Lawson, recently peddled the old myth (yet again) that "Karl Marx's view was that we are all mere creatures of economic determinism. What we do and what we think have nothing to do with personal autonomy. We are simply cogs in a class-war machine." Such cheap misrepresentations and distortions are pumped out on a daily basis in an attempt to discredit Marxism. However, Marx was never a vulgar economic determinist, where every action is reduced to simple economics. This is a complete distortion.

As Engels explained, "According to the materialist conception of history the determining element in history is *ultimately* the production and reproduction in real life. More than this neither Marx nor I have ever asserted. If therefore somebody twists this into the statement that the economic element is the *only* determining one, he transforms it into a meaningless, abstract and absurd phrase." Take note Mr. Lawson!

Engels went on: "The economic situation is the basis, but the various elements of the superstructure – political forms of the class struggle and its consequences, constitutions established by the victorious class after a successful battle, etc—forms of law—and then even the reflexes of all these actual struggles in the brains of the combatants: political, legal, philosophical theories, religious ideas and their further development into systems of dogma—also exercise their influence upon the course of the historical struggles and in many cases preponderate in determining their *form*. There is an interaction of all these elements, in which, amid all the endless *host* of accidents (i.e. of things and events whose inner connection is so remote or so impossible to prove that we regard it as absent and can neglect it), the economic movement finally asserts itself as necessary." (Engels to J. Bloch, 13 September 1890).

Trotsky also answers this nonsense: "On the question as to how the economic 'base' determines the political, juridical, philosophical, artistic and so on 'superstructure' there is a rich Marxist literature. The opinion that economics presumably determines directly and immediately the creativeness of a composer or even the verdict of a judge, represents a hoary caracature of Marxism which the bourgeois professordom of all countries has circulated time out of end to mask their intellectual impotence." (*In Defence of Marxism*).

Behind the bubbles

However, despite all the distortions and lies of our enemies, even these critics cannot help blurting out the truth once in a while. "Even so," says Professor Ferguson, "Marx's insights into capitalism can still illuminate... Marx got one thing right (!). Behind the bubbles and busts of the capitalist system there is a class struggle; and that class struggle is the key to modern politics." This is a bold admission from such a bias source. Normally, such ideas are strenously denied by all bourgeois apologists. Nevertheless, we should not get carried away, afterall, one swallow does not make a summer.

So what is this set of ideas that frightens the ruling class and its apologists so much? Put simply, Marxism, or Scientific Socialism, is the name given to the body of ideas first worked out by Karl Marx (1818-1883) and Friedrich Engels (1820-1895) more than 150 years ago. In essence, Marxism is a synthesis of the most advanced ideas at the time: English classical economics, German Hegelian philosophy and French socialism. In their totality, these ideas provide a fully worked-out theoretical basis for the struggle of the working class to attain a higher form of human society—socialism.

The component parts of Marxism fall under three main headings, corresponding broadly to philosophy, social history and economics—

Dialectical Materialism, Historical Materialism and Marxist Economics. These are the famous "Three sources and three component parts of Marxism" of which Lenin wrote.

The present book comprises the *Education for Socialists* series and other material which was launched a few years ago to promote the study of Marxism. They were originally intended to assist the student of Marxism by providing a basic introduction to the subject matter, with suitable Marxist texts, that we hoped would whet the appetite for further reading and study. This material, aimed at the first-time reader, is suitable for individual study or as the basis of Marxist discussion groups.

While these introductory articles are illuminating and provide a good start to the subject, there is no substitute for proceeding from there to tackle the classic works of Marx, Engels, Lenin, Trotsky, Plekhanov and others. The newer reader should not be put off by the sometimes difficult and abstract ideas expressed in these writings. Whatever the initial difficulty, a certain perseverance will pay just rewards. Marxism is a science with its own terminology, and therefore makes heavy demands upon the beginner. However, every serious person knows that nothing is worthwhile if attained without a degree of struggle and sacrifice, and that applies to Marxism as well.

The theories of Marxism provide the thinking worker and student with a comprehensive understanding of the world in which we live. It is the duty of those who wish to learn, to conquer for themselves the main theories of Marx and Engels, as an essential prerequisite for the overthrow of capitalism and the establishment of a socialist society.

Understand theory

We recognise that there are real obstacles in the path of ordinary workers in their struggle to understand theory. Yet it was for the working class that Marx and Engels wrote, and not for "clever" academics. As Engels explained: "If these gentlemen only knew how Marx thought his best things were still not good enough for the workers and how he regarded it as a crime to offer the workers anything less than the best!"

"Every beginning is difficult" no matter what science we are talking about. To the class conscious worker and the student who is prepared to persevere, one promise can be made: once the initial effort is made to come to grips with unfamiliar and new ideas, the theories of Marxism will be found to be basically straight-forward and simple. It will open your eyes to a new world, where the irrational workings of class society become clear. Once the basic concepts of Marxism are conquered, it introduces us to a whole new outlook on politics, the class struggle, and, in fact, every aspect of life.

Above all, Marxism is a *guide to action.* It prepares theoretically us for the struggle for a new society. These ideas will become the property of millions as the scientific programme of socialism connects with the revolutionary movement of the masses.

In the famous words of Marx, "Philosophers have interpreted the world; the point however is to change it."

Rob Sewell

September 2007

Dialectical Materialism

By Rob Sewell

Scientific socialism or Marxism is composed of three component parts: Dialectical Materialism, Historical Materialism and Marxist Economics. We begin with an explanation of the *method* of Marxism, namely Dialectical Materialism.

For those unacquainted with Marxist philosophy, dialectical materialism may seem an obscure and difficult concept. However, for those prepared to take the time to study this new way of looking at things, they will discover a revolutionary outlook that will allow them an insight into and understanding of the mysteries of the world in which we live. A grasp of dialectical materialism is an essential prerequisite in understanding the doctrine of Marxism. Dialectical materialism is the philosophy of Marxism, which provides us with a scientific and comprehensive world outlook. It is the philosophical bedrock—the method—on which the whole of Marxist doctrine is founded.

According to Engels, dialectics was "our best working tool and our sharpest weapon." And for us also, it is a guide to action and our activities within the working class movement. It is similar to a compass or map, which allows us to get our bearings in the turmoil of events, and permits us to understand the underlying processes that shape our world.

Whether we like it or not, consciously or unconsciously, everyone has a philosophy. A philosophy is simply a way of looking at the world. Under capitalism, without our own scientific philosophy, we will inevitably adopt the dominant philosophy of the ruling class and the prejudices of the society in which we live. "Things will never change" is a common refrain, reflecting the futility of changing things and of the need to accept our lot in life. There are other such proverbs as "There is nothing new under the sun", and "History always repeats itself", which reflect the same conservative outlook. Such ideas, explained Marx, form a crushing weight on the consciousness of men and women.

Just as the emerging bourgeoisie in its revolution against feudal society challenged the conservative ideas of the old feudal aristocracy, so the working class, in its fight for a new society, needs to challenge the dominant outlook of its own oppressor, the capitalist class. Of course, the ruling class, through its monopoly control of the mass media, the press, school, university and pulpit, consciously justifies its system of exploitation as the most "natural form of society". The repressive state machine, with its "armed bodies of men", is not sufficient to maintain the capitalist system. The dominant ideas and morality of bourgeois society serve as a vital defence of the material interests of the ruling class. Without this powerful ideology, the capitalist system could not last for any length of time.

"In one way or another", states Lenin, "all official and liberal science defends wage-slavery... To expect science to be impartial in a wage-slave society is as foolishly naïve as to expect impartiality from manufacturers on the question of whether workers' wages ought not to be increased by decreasing the profits of capital."

Official bourgeois ideology conducts a relentless war against Marxism, which it correctly sees as a mortal danger to capitalism. The bourgeois scribes and professors pour out a continual stream of propaganda in an attempt to discredit Marxism—particularly the dialectic. This has especially been the case since the collapse of the Berlin Wall, and the ferocious ideological offensive against Marxism, communism, revolution, and such like. "Marxism is dead", they repeatedly proclaim like some religious incantation. But Marxism refuses to lie down in front of these witch doctors! Marxism reflects the unconscious will of the working class to change society. Its fate is linked to that of the proletariat.

The apologists of capitalism, together with their shadows in the labour movement, constantly assert that their system is a natural and permanent form of society. On the other hand, the dialect asserts that nothing is permanent and all things perish in time. Such a revolutionary philosophy constitutes a profound threat to the capitalist system and therefore must be discredited at all cost. This explains the daily churning out of anti-Marxist propaganda. But each real step forward in science and knowledge serves to confirm the correctness of the dialectic. For millions of people the growing crisis of capitalism increasingly demonstrates the validity of Marxism. The objective situation is forcing working people to seek a way out of the impasse. "Life teaches", remarked Lenin. Today, to use the famous words of the *Communist Manifesto*, "A spectre is haunting Europe, the spectre of communism."

In the fight for the emancipation of the working class, Marxism also wages a relentless war against capitalism and its ideology, which defends and justifies its system of exploitation, the "market economy". But Marxism does more than this. Marxism provides the working class with "an integral world outlook irreconcilable with any form of superstition, reaction, or defence of bourgeois oppression" (Lenin). It seeks to reveal the real relationships that exist under capitalism and arms the working class with an understanding of how it can achieve its own emancipation. Dialectical materialism, to use the words of the Russian Marxist Plekhanov, is more than an outlook, it is a "philosophy of action".

Men and women attempt to think in a rational manner. Logic (from the Greek *logos*, meaning word or reason) is the science of the laws of thinking. Whatever thoughts we think, and whatever language they are expressed in, they must satisfy the requirements of reasoning. These requirements give rise to laws of thought, to the principles of logic. It was the Greek philosopher Aristotle (384 - 322BC) more than 2,000 years ago who formulated the present system of formal logic—a system that is the basis of our educational establishments to this very day. He categorised the method of how we should reason correctly and how statements are combined to arrive at judgements, and from them, how conclusions are drawn. He laid down three basic laws of logic: the principle of Identity (A = A), of contradiction (A cannot be A and not-A), and the excluded middle (A is either A or non-A; there is no middle alternative).

Formal logic has held sway for more than two millennia and was the basis of experiment and the great advances of modern science. The development of mathematics was based on this logic. You cannot teach a child to add up without it. One plus one equals two, not three. Formal logic may seem like common sense and is responsible for the execution of a million and one everyday things, but—and this is the big but—it has its limits. When dealing with drawn out processes or complicated events, formal logic becomes a totally inadequate way of thinking. This is particularly the case in dealing with movement, change and contradiction. Formal logic regards things as fixed and motionless. Of course, this is not to deny the everyday usefulness of formal logic—on the contrary—but we need to recognise it limits.

"The dialectic is neither fiction nor mysticism," wrote Leon Trotsky, "but a science of the forms of our thinking insofar as it is not limited to the daily problems of life but attempts to arrive at an understanding of more complicated and drawn-out processes. The dialectic and formal logic bear a relationship similar to that between higher and lower mathematics." (*The ABC of Materialist Dialectics*).

With the development of modern science, the system of classification (of Linnaeus) was based on formal logic, where all living things were divided into species and orders. This constituted a great leap forward for biology compared to the past. However, it was a fixed and rigid system, with its rigid categories, which over time revealed its limits. Darwin in particular showed that through evolution it was possible for one species to be transformed into another species. Consequently, the rigid system of classification had to be changed to allow for this new understanding of reality.

In effect, the system of formal logic broke down. It could not cope with these contradictions. On the other hand, dialectics—the logic of change—explains that there are no absolute or fixed categories in nature or society. Engels had great fun in pointing to the duck-billed platypus, this transitional form, and asking where it fitted into the rigid scheme of things!

Only dialectical materialism can explain the laws of evolution and change, which sees the world not as a complex of ready-made things, but as a complex of processes, which go through an uninterrupted transformation of coming into being and passing away. For Hegel, the old logic was exactly like a child's game, which sought to make pictures out of jigsaw pieces. "The fundamental flaw in vulgar thought", wrote Trotsky, "lies in the fact that it wishes to content itself with motionless imprints of reality which consists of eternal motion."

Before we look at the main laws of dialectical materialism, let us take a look at the origins of the materialist outlook.

Materialism versus idealism

"The philosophy of Marxism is materialism", wrote Lenin. Philosophy itself fits into two great ideological camps: materialism and idealism. Before we proceed, even these terms need an explanation. To begin with, materialism and idealism have nothing whatsoever in common with their everyday usage, where materialism is associated with material greed and swindling (in short, the morality of present-day capitalism) and idealism with high ideals and virtue. Far from it!

Philosophical materialism is the outlook which explains that there is only one material world. There is no Heaven or Hell. The universe, which has always existed and is not the creation of any supernatural being, is in the process of constant flux. Human beings are a part of nature, and evolved from lower forms of life, whose origins sprung from a lifeless planet some 3.6 billion or so years ago. With the evolution of life, at a certain stage, came the development of animals with a nervous system, and eventually human beings with a large brain. With humans emerged human thought and consciousness. The human brain alone is capable of producing general ideas, i.e. thinking. Therefore matter, which existed eternally, has always existed independently of the mind and human beings. Things existed long before any awareness of them arose or could have arisen on the part of living organisms.

For materialists there is no consciousness apart from the living brain, which is part of a material body. A mind without a body is an absurdity. Matter is not a product of mind, but mind itself is the highest product of matter. Ideas are simply a reflection of the independent material world that surrounds us. Things reflected in a mirror do not depend on this reflection for their existence. "All ideas are taken from experience, are reflections—true or distorted—of reality," states Engels. Or to use the words of Marx, "Life is not determined by consciousness, but consciousness by life".

Marxists do not deny that mind, consciousness, thought, will, feeling or sensation are real. What materialists deny is that the thing called "the mind" exists separately from the body. Mind is not distinct from the body. Thinking is the product of the brain, which is the organ of thought.

Yet this does not mean that our consciousness is a lifeless mirror of nature. Human beings relate to their surroundings; they are aware of their surroundings and react accordingly; in turn, the environment reacts back upon them. While rooted in material conditions, human beings generalise and think creatively. They in turn change their material surroundings.

On the other hand, philosophical idealism states that the material world is not real but is simply the reflection of the world of ideas. There are different forms of idealism, but all essentially explain that ideas are primary and matter, if it exists at all, secondary. For the idealists, ideas are dissevered from matter, from nature. This is Hegel's conception of the Absolute Idea or what amounts to God. Philosophical idealism opens the road, in one way or another, to the defence of or support for religion and superstition. Not only is this outlook false, it is also profoundly conservative, leading us to the pessimistic conclusion that we can never understand the "mysterious ways" of the world. Whereas materialism understands that human beings not only observe the real world, but can change it, and in doing so, change themselves.

The idealist view of the world grew out of the division of labour between physical and mental labour. This division constituted an enormous advance as it freed a section of society from physical work and allowed them the time to develop science and technology. However, the further they were removed from physical labour, the more abstract became their ideas. And when thinkers separate their ideas from the real world, they become increasingly consumed by abstract "pure thought" and end up with all types of fantasies. Today, cosmology is dominated by complex abstract mathematical conceptions, which have led to all sorts of weird and wonderful erroneous theories: the Big Bang, beginning of time, parallel universes, etc. Every break with practice leads to a one-sided idealism.

The materialist outlook has a long history stretching back to the ancient Greeks of Anaxagoras (c.500 - 428 BC) and Democritus (c.460 - c.370 BC). With the collapse of Ancient Greece, this rational outlook was cut across for a whole historical epoch, and only after the reawakening of thought following the demise of the Christian Middle Ages was there a revival of philosophy and natural science. From the seventeenth century, the home of modern materialism was England. "The real progenitor of English materialism is Bacon," wrote Marx. The materialism of Francis Bacon (1561 - 1626) was then systemised and developed by Thomas Hobbes (1588 - 1679), whose ideas were in turn developed by John Locke (1632 - 1704). The latter already thought it possible that matter could posses the faculty of thinking. It is no accident that these advances in human thought coincided with the rise of the bourgeoisie and great advances in science, particularly mechanics, astronomy and medicine. These great thinkers in turn provided the breakthrough for the brilliant school of French materialists of the eighteenth century, most notably René Descartes (1596 - 1650).

It was their materialism and rationalism that became the creed of the Great French Revolution of 1789. These revolutionary thinkers recognised no external authority. Everything from religion to natural science, from society to political institutions, was subjected to the most searching criticism. Reason became the measure of everything.

This materialist philosophy, consistently championed by Holbach (1723 - 1789) and Helvetius, was a revolutionary philosophy. "The universe is the vast unity of everything that is, everywhere it shows us only matter in movement," states Holbach. "This is all that there is and it displays only an infinite and continuous chain of causes and actions; some of these causes we know, since they immediately strike our senses; others we do not know since they act on us only by means of consequences, quite remote from first causes."

This rational philosophy was an ideological reflection of the revolutionary bourgeoisie's struggle against the church, the aristocracy and the absolute monarchy. It represented a fierce attack on the ideology of the Old Order. In the end, the kingdom of Reason became nothing more than the idealised kingdom of the bourgeoisie. Bourgeois property became one of the essential rights of man. The revolutionary materialists paved the way for the new bourgeois society and the domination of new forms of private property. "Different times, different circumstances, a different philosophy," stated Denis Diderot (1713 - 1784).

The new materialism, although a revolutionary advance, tended to be very rigid and mechanical. These new philosophers attacked the church and denied the self-sufficiency of the soul and held that man was simply a material body as all other animals and inorganic bodies. Man was regarded as a more complex and more delicate mechanism than other bodies. According to La Mettrie (1709 - 1751) in his principal work *Man the Machine*, "We are instruments endowed with feeling and memory."

For the French materialists the origin of knowledge—the discovery of objective truth—lay through the action of nature on our senses. The planets and man's place within the solar system and nature itself was fixed. For them, it was a clockwork world, where everything had its logical static place, and where the impulse for movement came from outside. The whole approach, while materialist, was mechanical, and failed to grasp the living reality of the world. It could not grasp the universe as a process, as matter undergoing continuous change. This weakness led to the false dichotomy between the material world and the world of ideas. And this dualism opened the door to idealism.

Others held to a monist view that the universe was one system which was not pure spirit or pure matter. Spinoza was the first to work out such a system. While he saw the need for a God, the universe was one system, which was wholly material from end to end.

Dialectics and Metaphysics

The Marxist view of the world is not only materialist, but also dialectical. For its critics, the dialectic is portrayed as something totally mystical, and therefore irrelevant. But this is certainly not the case. The dialectical method is simply an attempt to understand more clearly our real interdependent world. Dialectics, states Engels in *Anti-Duhring*, "is nothing more than the science of the general laws of motion and development of nature, human society and thought." Put simply, it is the logic of motion.

It is obvious to most people that we do not live in a static world. In fact, everything in nature is in a state of constant change. "Motion is the mode of existence of matter," states Engels. "Never anywhere has there been matter without motion, nor can there be." The earth revolves continually around its axis, and in turn itself revolves around the sun. This results in day and night, and the different seasons that we experience throughout the year. We are born, grow up, grow old and eventually die. Everything is moving, changing, either rising and developing or declining and dying away. Any equilibrium is only relative, and only has meaning in relation to other forms of motion.

"When we consider and reflect upon nature at large or the history of mankind or our own intellectual activity, at first we see the picture of an endless entanglement of relations and reactions, permutations and combinations, in which nothing remains what, where, and as it was, but everything moves, changes, comes into being, and passes away," remarks Engels. "We see, therefore, at first the picture as a whole, with its individual parts still more or less kept in the background; we observe the movements, transitions, connections rather than the things that move, combine, and are connected. This primitive, naïve but intrinsically correct conception of the world is that of ancient Greek philosophy, and was first clearly formulated by Heraclitus: everything is and is not, for everything is fluid, is constantly changing, constantly coming into being and passing away."

The Greeks made a whole series of revolutionary discoveries and advances in natural science. Anaximander made a map of the world, and wrote a book on cosmology, from which only a few fragments survive. The Antikythera mechanism, as it is called, appears to be the remains of a clockwork planetarium dating back to the first century BC. Given the limited knowledge of the time, many were anticipations and inspired guesses. Under slave society, these brilliant inventions could not be put to productive use and were simply regarded as playthings for amusement. The real advances in natural science took place in the mid-fifteenth century. The new methods of investigation meant the division of nature into its individual parts, allowing objects and processes to be classified. While this provided massive amounts of data, objects were analysed in isolation and not in their living environment. This produced a narrow, rigid, metaphysical mode of thought that has become the hallmark of empiricism. "The Facts" became the all important feature. "Now, what I want is, Facts. Teach these boys and girls nothing but Facts. Facts alone are wanted in life," states the Dickensian character Thomas Gradgrind in *Hard Times*.

"To the metaphysician things and their mental reflexes, ideas, are isolated, are to be considered one after the other and apart from each other, are objects of investigation fixed, rigid, given once and for all", states Engels. "He thinks in absolutely irreconcilable antitheses. 'His communication is "yea, yea; nay, nay"; for whatsoever is more than these cometh of evil.' For him a thing either exists or does not exist; a thing cannot at the same time be itself and something else. Positive and negative absolutely exclude one another; cause and effect stand in rigid antithesis one to another.

"At first sight this mode of thinking seems to us very luminous, because it is that of so-called sound common sense. Only sound common sense, respectable fellow that he is, in the homely realm of his own four walls, has very wonderful adventures directly he ventures out into the wide world of research. And the metaphysical mode of thought, justifiable and necessary as it is in a number of domains whose extent varies according to the nature of the particular object of investigation, sooner or later reaches a limit beyond which it becomes one-sided, restricted, abstract, lost in insoluble contradictions. In the contemplation of individual things it forgets the connection between them; in the contemplation of their existence it forgets the beginning and the end of that existence; of their repose, it forgets their motion. It cannot see the wood for the trees."

Engels goes on to explain that for everyday purposes we know whether an animal is alive or not. But upon closer examination, we are forced to recognise that is not a simple straightforward question. On the contrary, it is a complex question. There are raging debates even today as to when life begins in the mothers' womb. Likewise, it is just as difficult to say when the exact moment of death occurs, as physiology proves that death is not a single instantaneous act, but a protracted process. In the brilliant words of the Greek philosopher Heraclitus, "It is the same thing in us that is living and dead, asleep and awake, young and old; each changes place and becomes the other. We step and we do not step into the same stream; we are and we are not."

Not everything is as appears on the surface of things. Every species, every aspect of organic life, is every moment the same and not the same. It develops by assimilating matter from without and simultaneously discards other unwanted matter; continually some cells die, while others are renewed. Over time, the body is completely transformed, renewed from top to bottom. Therefore, every organic entity is both itself and yet something other than itself.

This phenomenon cannot be explained by metaphysical thought or formal logic. This approach is incapable of explaining contradiction. This contradictory reality does not enter the realm of common sense reasoning. Dialectics, on the other hand, comprehends things in their connection, development, and motion. As far as Engels was concerned, "Nature is the proof of dialectics."

Here is how Engels described the rich processes of change in his book the *Dialectics of Nature*:

"Matter moves in an eternal cycle, completing its trajectory in a period so vast that in comparison with it our earthly year is as nothing; in a cycle in which the period of highest development, namely the period of organic life with its crowning achievement - self-consciousness, is a space just as comparatively minute in the history of life and self-consciousness; in a cycle in which every particular form of the existence of matter - be it the sun or a nebular, a particular animal or animal-species, a chemical combination or decomposition - is equally in transition; in a cycle in which nothing is eternal, except eternally changing, eternally moving matter and the laws of its movement and change. But however often and pitilessly this cycle may be accomplished in time and space, however many countless suns and earths may arise and fall, however long it may be necessary to wait until in some solar system, on some planet appear conditions suitable for organic life, however many countless beings may fall and rise before, out of their midst, develop animals with a thinking brain that find an environment that permits them to live, be it even only for a short period, we are, nevertheless, assured that matter in all its changes remains eternally one and the same, that not one of its attributes may perish, and that that same iron necessity which compels the destruction of the highest early bloom of matter—the thinking spirit—also necessitates its rebirth at some other place, at some other time."

Along with, and following the French philosophy of the eighteenth century, arose a new radical German philosophy. Through Emmanuel Kant, the culmination of this philosophy was epitomised by the system of George F. Hegel, who had greatly admired the French Revolution. Hegel, although an idealist, was the most encyclopaedic mind of his age. The great contribution of this genius was the rescuing of the dialectical mode of thought originally developed by the ancient Greek philosophers some 2,000 years before.

"Changes in being consist not only in the fact that one quantity passes into another quantity, but also that quality passes into quantity, and vice versa," wrote Hegel. "Each transition of the latter kind represents an interruption, and gives the phenomenon a new aspect, qualitatively distinct from the previous one. Thus water when cooled grows hard, not gradually... but all at once; having already cooled to freezing-point, it can still remain a liquid only if preserves a tranquil condition, and then the slightest shock is sufficient for it suddenly to become hard... In the world of moral phenomena... there take place the same changes of quantitative into qualitative, and differences in qualities there also are founded upon quantitative differences. Thus, a little less, a little more constitutes that limit beyond which frivolity ceases and there appears something quite different, crime..." (*The Science of Logic*).

Hegel's works are full of references and examples of dialectics. Unfortunately, Hegel was not only an idealist, but wrote in the most obscure and abstruse fashion imaginable, making his works very difficult to read. Lenin, while re-reading Hegel in exile during the First World War, wrote: "I am in general trying to read Hegel materialistically: Hegel is materialism which has been stood on its head (according to Engels) - that is to say, I cast aside for the most part God, the Absolute, the Pure Idea, etc." Lenin was greatly impressed by Hegel, and, despite his idealism, later recommended that young communists study his writings for themselves.

The young Marx and Engels were followers of the great Hegel. They learned a colossal amount from this teacher. He opened their eyes to a new outlook on the world epitomised by the dialectic. By embracing the dialectic, Hegel freed history from metaphysics. For the dialectic, there is nothing final, absolute, or sacred. It reveals the transitory character of everything. However, Hegel was limited by his knowledge, the knowledge of his age, and the fact he was an idealist. He regarded thoughts within the brain not as more or less abstract pictures of real things and processes, but as realisations of the "Absolute Idea", existing from eternity. Hegel's idealism turned reality on its head.

Nevertheless, Hegel systematically outlined the important laws of change, touched upon earlier.

The law of quantity into quality (and vice versa)

"It has been said that there are no sudden leaps in nature, and it is a common notion that things have their origin through gradual increase or decrease," states Hegel. "But there is also such a thing as sudden transformation from quantity to quality. For example, water does not become gradually hard on cooling, becoming first pulpy and ultimately attaining a rigidity of ice, but turns hard at once. If temperature be lowered to a certain degree, the water is suddenly changed into ice, i.e., the quantity—the number of degrees of temperature—is transformed into quality—a change in the nature of the thing." (*The Science of Logic*).

This is the cornerstone of understanding change. Change or evolution does not take place gradually in a straight smooth line. Marx compared the social revolution to an old mole burrowing busily beneath the ground, invisible for long periods, but steadily undermining the old order and later emerging into the light in a sudden overturn. Even Charles Darwin believed that his theory of evolution was essentially gradual and that the gaps in the fossil record did not represent any breaks or leaps in evolution, and would be "filled in" by further discoveries. In this Darwin was wrong. Today, new theories, essentially dialectical, have been put forward to explain the leaps in evolution. Stephen J. Gould and Niles Eldredge termed their dialectical theory of evolution "punctuated equilibria". They explained that there were long periods of evolution where there were no apparent changes taking place, then suddenly, a new life form or forms emerged. In other words, quantitative differences gave rise to a qualitative change, leading to new species. The whole of development is characterised by breaks in continuity, leaps, catastrophes and revolutions.

The emergence of single-cellular life in the earth's oceans some 3.6 billion years ago was a qualitative leap in the evolution of matter. The

"Cambrian explosion", some 600 million years ago, where complex multi-cellular life with hard parts exploded onto the scene was a further qualitative leap forward in evolution. In the lower Palaeozoic, some 400 to 500 million years ago, the first vertebrate fish emerged. This revolutionary design became dominant and advanced through the amphibians (which lived both in water and on land), through reptiles, and finally branched off into warm-blooded creatures: birds and mammals. Such revolutionary leaps culminated in human beings that have the capacity to think. Evolution is a long process whereby an accumulation of changes inside and outside the organism leads to a leap, a qualitatively higher state of development.

Just as colossal subterranean pressures that accumulate and periodically break through the earth's crust in the form of earthquakes, so gradual changes in the consciousness of workers lead to an explosion in the class struggle. A strike in a factory is not caused by outside "agitators", but is produced by an accumulation of changes within the factory that finally pushes the workforce to strike. The "cause" of the strike maybe something quite small and incidental, a tea-break for instance, but it has become "the last straw that breaks the camel's back", to use a popular (dialectical) expression. It has become the catalyst whereby quantity changes into quality.

Today, a whole series of left wing electoral victories within the British trade unions are a product of a long accumulation of discontent within the union rank and file. Twenty years of bitter attacks on the working class has resulted in these changes at the top of the trade unions. Only those armed with a Marxist philosophy could foresee this development, which is rooted in the changing objective situation. These changes of mood, which are already taking place in the trade unions, will inevitably be reflected within the Labour Party at a certain stage that will result in the demise of the right wing under Blair. The ultra-lefts on the fringes of the Labour movement have continually written off the Labour Party as something that could never be changed. They are incapable of thinking dialectically, and have an empirical and formalistic outlook that only sees the surface of reality. They fail to draw a distinction between appearance and reality—between the immediate appearance evident to observation and the hidden processes, interconnections and laws that underlie the observed facts. In other words, they are blind to the subterranean processes taking place before their very eyes. "Blairism dominates the Labour Party!" they exclaim and throw up their hands in despair. They are under the spell of formal logic, and do not understand the process at work that will inevitably undermine Blairism, and lead to its collapse, as night follows day. As they wrote off the right wing unions in the past, they write off the Labour Party today. On the basis of events and the pressures of the leftward moving trade union movement, the Labour Party, given its roots in the trade unions, will inevitably move in a similar direction.

Marx stressed that the task of science is always to proceed from the immediate knowledge of appearances to the discovery of reality, of the essence, of the laws underlying the appearances. Marx's *Capital* is a fine example of this method. "The way of thinking of the vulgar economists", wrote Marx to Engels, "derives from the fact that it is always only the immediate form in which relationships appear which is reflected in the brain, and not their inner connections." (June 27, 1867).

The same could be said of those who in the past wrote off the Soviet Union as "state capitalist". Stalinism had nothing in common with socialism; it was a repressive regime, where workers had less rights than in the west. However, instead of a scientific analysis of the Soviet Union, they simply pronounced it state capitalist. As Trotsky explained the theorists of state capitalism looked at the USSR through the eyes of formal logic. It was either-or, black or white. The USSR was either a wonderful socialist state, as the Stalinists said, or it must be a (state) capitalist state. Such thinking is pure formalism. They never understood the possibility of a degeneration of the workers' state into a chronically deformed variant of proletarian rule, as explained by Trotsky. It is clear that the revolution, due to its isolation in a backward country, went through a process of degeneration. However, while the nationalised planned economy remained, not everything was lost. The bureaucracy was not a new ruling class with a historic mission, but a parasitic growth on the state, which usurped political power. Only a new political revolution could eliminate the bureaucracy and reintroduce soviets and workers' democracy.

As Trotsky explained just before his death: "The definition of the USSR given by comrade Burnham, 'not a workers' state and not a bourgeois state,' is purely negative, wrenched from the chain of historical development, left dangling in mid-air, void of a single particle of sociology and represents simply a theoretical capitulation of pragmatism before a contradictory historical phenomenon.

"If Burnham were a dialectical materialist, he would have probed the following three questions: (1) What is the historical origin of the USSR? (2) What changes has this state suffered during its existence? (3) Did these changes pass from the quantitative stage to the qualitative? That is, did they create a historically necessary domination by a new exploiting class? Answering these questions would have forced Burnham to draw the only possible conclusion - the USSR is still a degenerated workers' state." (*In Defence of Marxism*).

The supporters of state capitalism tied themselves in knots, confusing counterrevolution with revolution and vice versa. In Afghanistan, they supported the reactionary fundamentalist mujahideen as "freedom fighters" against Russian "imperialism". With the collapse of the USSR and the move to restore capitalism from 1991 onwards, they remained neutral in face of real capitalist counterrevolution.

The Unity of Opposites

"The contradiction, however, is the source of all movement and life; only in so far as it contains a contradiction can anything have movement, power, and effect." (Hegel). "In brief", states Lenin, "dialectics can be defined as the doctrine of the unity of opposites. This embodies the essence of dialectics..."

The world in which we live is a unity of contradictions or a unity of opposites: cold-heat, light-darkness, Capital-Labour, birth-death, riches-poverty, positive-negative, boom-slump, thinking-being, finite-infinite, repulsion-attraction, left-right, above-below, evolution-revolution, chance-necessity, sale-purchase, and so on.

The fact that two poles of a contradictory antithesis can manage to coexist as a whole is regarded in popular wisdom as a paradox. The paradox is a recognition that two contradictory, or opposite, considerations may both be true. This is a reflection in thought of a unity of opposites in the material world.

Motion, space and time are nothing else but the mode of existence of matter. Motion, as we have explained is a contradiction, being in one place and another at the same time. It is a unity of opposites. "Movement means to be in this place and not to be in it; this is the continuity of space and time—and it is this which first makes motion possible." (Hegel)

To understand something, its essence, it is necessary to seek out these internal contradictions. Under certain circumstances, the universal is the individual, and the individual is the universal. That things turn into their opposites - cause can become effect and effect can become cause - is because they are merely links in the never-ending chain in the development of matter.

"The negative is to an equal extent positive," states Hegel. Dialectical thought is "comprehending the antithesis in its unity." In fact Hegel goes further: "Contradiction is the root of all movement and vitality, and it is only insofar as it contains a Contradiction that anything moves and has impulse and activity... Something moves, not because it is here at one point of time and there at another, but because at one and the same point of time it is here and not here, and in this here both is and is not. We must grant the old dialecticians the contradictions which they prove in motion; but what follows is not that there is no motion, but rather that motion is existent Contradiction itself." Therefore for Hegel, something is living insofar as it contains contradiction, which provides it with self-movement.

The Greek atomists first advanced the revolutionary theory that the material world was made up of atoms, considered the smallest unit of matter. The Greek word *atomos* means indivisible. This was a brilliant intuitive guess. Twentieth century science proved that everything was composed of atoms, although it was subsequently discovered that even smaller particles existed. Every atom contains a nucleus at its centre, composed of sub-atomic particles called protons and neutrons. Surrounding the nucleus are particles known as electrons. All protons carry a positive electrical charge, and would therefore repel each other, but they are bound together by a type of energy known as the strong nuclear force. This shows that everything that exists is based on a unity of opposites and has self-movement of "impulse and activity", to use Hegel's words.

In humans, the level of blood sugar is essential for life. Too high a level is likely to result in diabetic coma, too little and the person is incapable of eating. This safe level is regulated by the rate at which sugar is released into the bloodstream by the digestion of carbohydrates, the rate at which stored glycogen, fat or protein is converted into sugar, and the rate at which sugar is removed and utilised. If the blood sugar level rises, then the rate of utilisation is increased by the release of more insulin from the pancreas. If it falls, more sugar is released into the blood, or the person gets hungry and consumes a source of sugar. In this self-regulation of opposing forces, of positive and negative feedbacks, the blood level is kept within tolerable limits.

Lenin explains this self-movement in a note when he says, "Dialectics is the teaching which shows how opposites can be and how they become identical - under what conditions they are identical, becoming transformed into one another - why the human mind should grasp these opposites not as dead, rigid, but living, conditional, mobile, becoming transformed into one another."

Lenin also laid great stress on the importance of contradiction as the motive force of development. "It is common knowledge that, in any given society, the strivings of some of its members conflict with the strivings of others, that social life is full of contradictions, and that history reveals a struggle between nations and societies, as well as within nations and societies, and, besides, an alternation of periods of revolution and reaction, peace and war, stagnation and rapid progress or decline." (Lenin, *Three Sources and Component Parts of Marxism*).

This is best illustrated by the class struggle. Capitalism requires a capitalist class and a working class. The struggle over the surplus value created by the workers and expropriated by the capitalists leads to an irreconcilable struggle that will provide the basis for the eventual overthrow of capitalism, and the resolution of the contradiction through the abolition of classes.

The Negation of the Negation

The general pattern of historical development is not one of a straight line upward, but of a complex interaction in which each step forward is only achieved at the cost of a partial step backwards. These regressions, in turn, are remedied at the next stage of development.

The law of the negation of the negation explains the repetition at a higher level of certain features and properties of the lower level and the apparent return of past features. There is a constant struggle between form and content and between content and form, resulting in the eventual shattering of the old form and the transformation of the content.

This whole process can be best pictured as a spiral, where the movement comes back to the position it started, but at a higher level. In other words, historical progress is achieved through a series of contradictions. Where the previous stage is negated, this does not represent its total elimination. It does not wipe out completely the stage that it supplants.

"The capitalist method of appropriation, which springs from the capitalist method of production, and therefore capitalist private property, is the first negation of individual private property based on one's own labour. But capitalist production begets with the inevitableness of a natural process its own negation. It is the negation of the negation," remarked Marx in volume one of *Capital*.

Engels explains a whole series of examples to illustrate the negation of the negation in his book *Anti-Duhring*. "Let us take a grain of barley. Millions of such grains of barley are milled, boiled and brewed and then consumed. But if such a grain of barley meets with conditions which for it are normal, if it falls on suitable soil, then under the influence of heat and moisture a specific change takes place, it germinates; the grain as such ceases to exist, it is negated, and in its place appears the plant which has arisen from it, the negation of the grain. But what is the normal life-process of this plant? It grows, flowers, is fertilised and finally once more produces grains of barley, and, as soon as these have ripened, the stalk dies, and is in its turn negated. As a result of this negation of the negation we have once again the original grain of barley, but not as a single unit, but ten, twenty or thirty fold."

The barley lives and evolves by means of returning to its starting point —but at a higher level. One seed has produced many. Also over time, plants have evolved qualitatively as well as quantitatively. Successive generations have shown variations, and become more adapted to their environment.

Engels gives a further example from the insect world. "Butterflies, for example, spring from the egg through a negation of the egg, they pass through certain transformations until they reach sexual maturity, they pair and are in turn negated, dying as soon as the pairing process has been completed and the female has laid its numerous eggs."

Hegel and Marx

Hegel, who had a giant intellect, illuminated a great many things. It was a debt that Marx repeatedly recognised. "The mystification which dialectic suffers in Hegel's hands, by no means prevents him from being the first to present its general form of working in a comprehensive and conscious manner," states Marx. Nevertheless, Hegel's philosophical system was a huge miscarriage. It suffered from an incurable internal contradiction. Hegel's conception of history is an evolutionary one, where there is nothing final or eternal. However, his system laid claim to being the absolute truth, in complete contradiction to the laws of dialectical thought. While Hegel defended the status quo in Germany, the dialectic embraced a revolutionary view of constant change. For Hegel, all that was real was rational. But using the Hegelian dialectic, all that is real will become irrational. All that exists deserves to perish. In this lay the revolutionary significance of the Hegelian philosophy.

The solution of this contradiction led back to materialism, but not the old mechanical materialism, but one based upon the new sciences and advances. "Materialism rose again enriched by all the acquisitions of idealism. The most important of these acquisitions was the dialectical method, the examination of phenomena in their development, in their origin and destruction. The genius who represented this new direction of thought was Karl Marx," writes Plekhanov. Spurred on by revolutionary developments in Europe in 1830-31, the Hegelian School split into left, right and centre.

The most prominent representative of the Hegelian Left was Ludwig Feuerbach, who challenged the old orthodoxy, especially religion, and placed materialism at the centre of things again. "Nature has no beginning and no end. Everything in it is in mutual interaction, everything at once effect and cause, everything in it is all-sided and reciprocal..." writes Feuerbach, adding that there is no place there for God. "Christians tear out the spirit, the soul, of man out of his body and make this torn-out, disembodied spirit into their God." Despite Feuerbach's limitations, Marx and Engels welcomed the new breakthrough with enthusiasm.

"But in the meantime", noted Engels, "the Revolution of 1848 thrust the whole of philosophy aside as unceremoniously as Feuerbach himself was also pushed into the background." It was left to Marx and Engels to consistently apply the dialectic to the new materialism, producing dialectical materialism. For them, the new philosophy was not an abstract philosophy, but directly linked to practice.

"Dialectics reduces itself to the science of the general laws of motion, both of the external world and of human thought—two sets of laws which are identical in substance, but differ in their expression in so far as the human mind can apply them consciously, while in nature and also up to now for the most part in human history, these laws assert themselves unconsciously, in the form of external necessity, in the midst of an endless series of seeming accidents." (Engels)

Neither Marx nor Engels left behind them a comprehensive book on dialectics as such. Marx was preoccupied with *Capital*. Engels intended to write such a book, but was overtaken by the need to complete Capital after Marx's death. He nevertheless wrote quite extensively on the subject, especially in *Anti-Dühring* and the *Dialectics of Nature*. Lenin commentated, "If Marx did not leave behind him a 'Logic' (with a capital letter), he did leave the *logic of Capital*, and this ought to be utilised to the full. In *Capital*, Marx applied to a single science logic, dialectics and the theory of knowledge of materialism (three words are not needed: it is one and the same thing) which has taken everything valuable in Hegel and developed it further."

Today, a small number of scientists, mainly from the natural sciences, have become conscious of the dialectic, which has opened their eyes to problems in their specialised fields. This relationship between science and dialectical materialism has been fully discussed in the book by Alan Woods and Ted Grant *Reason in Revolt*. They showed, along with Engels, that nature is completely dialectical. Apart from Stephen J. Gould and Niles Eldredge, Richard Levins and Richard Lewontin, who regard themselves as dialectical materialists, have written about the application of the dialectic to the field of biology in their book *The Dialectical Biologist:*

"What characterises the dialectical world, in all its aspects, as we have described it is that it is constantly in motion. Constants become variables, causes become effects, and systems develop, destroying the conditions that gave rise to them. Even elements that appear to be stable are in a dynamic equilibrium of forces that can suddenly become unbalanced, as when a dull grey lump of metal of a critical size becomes a fireball brighter than a thousand suns. Yet the motion is not unconstrained and uniform. Organisms develop and differentiate, then die and disintegrate. Species arise but inevitably become extinct. Even in the simple physical world we know of no uniform motion. Even the earth rotating on its axis has slowed down in geological time. The development of systems through time, then, seems to be the consequence of opposing forces and opposing motions.

"This appearance of opposing forces has given rise to the most debated and difficult, yet the most central, concept in dialectical thought, the principle of contradiction. For some, contradiction is an epistemic principle only. It describes how we come to understand the world by a history of antithetical theories that, in contradiction to each other and in contradiction to observed phenomena, lead to a new view of nature. Kuhn's (1962) theory of scientific revolution has some of this flavour of continual contradiction and resolution, giving way to new contradiction. For others, contradiction becomes an ontological property at least of human social existence. For us, contradiction is not only epistemic and political, but also ontological in the broadest sense. Contradictions between forces are everywhere in nature, not only in human social institutions. This tradition of dialectics goes back to Engels (1880) who wrote, in *Dialectics of Nature*, that 'to me there could be no question of building the laws of dialectics of nature, but of discovering them in it and evolving them from it.'" (*The Dialectical Biologist,* p.279).

Marxists have always stressed the unity of theory and practice. "Philosophers have only interpreted the world, in various ways; the point, however, is to change it", as Marx pointed to in his *Thesis on Feuerbach.* "If the truth is abstract it must be untrue," states Hegel. All truth is concrete. We have to look at things as they exist, with a view to understanding their underlying contradictory development. This has very important conclusions, especially for those fighting to change society. Unlike the Utopian socialists who viewed socialism as a wonderful idea, Marxists see the development of socialism as arising out of the contradictions of capitalism. Capitalist society has prepared the material basis for a classless society with its highly developed productive forces and its world division of labour. It has brought into being the working class, whose very life existence brings it into conflict with capitalism. On the basis of experience, it will become fully conscious of its position in society and it will be transformed, in the words of Marx, from a "class in-itself" to a "class for-itself".

Dialectics bases itself on determinism, but this has nothing in common with *fatalism* which denies the existence of accident in nature, society and thought. Dialectical determinism asserts the unity of necessity and accident, and explains that necessity expresses itself through accident. All events have causes, necessary events and accidental ones alike. If there were no causal laws in nature everything would be in a state of utter chaos. It would be an impossible position where nothing could exist. So everything is dependent upon everything else, as in a continuous chain of cause and effect. Particular events always have a chance or accidental character, but these arise only as the result of a deeper necessity. In fact, necessity manifests itself through a series of accidents. Without doubt, accidents have their place, but the essential thing is to discover what laws determine this deeper necessity.

From the point of view of superficial observation, everything may appear to be accidental or open to chance. This can appear especially so when we have no knowledge of the laws that govern change and their interconnections. "Where on the surface accident holds sway, there actually it is always governed by inner, hidden laws and it is only a matter of discovering these laws," remarked Engels in *Ludwig Feuerbach*.

In nature, the evolution of matter follows a certain path, although how, when, and in what form this is realised, depends upon accidental circumstances. For example, whether life was created or not on earth depended on a whole series of accidental factors, such as the presence of water, different chemical elements, the earth's distance from the sun, an atmosphere, etc. "It is the nature of matter to advance to the evolution of thinking beings", states Engels, "hence, too, this always necessarily occurs whenever the conditions for it (not necessarily identical at all places and times) are present... what is maintained to be necessary is composed of sheer accidents, and the so-called accidental is the form behind which necessity hides itself."

Superficial historians have written that the First World War was "caused" by the assassination of a Crown Prince at Sarajevo. To a Marxist this event was an historical accident, in the sense that this chance event served as the pretext, or catalyst, for the world conflict which had already been made inevitable by the economic, political and military contradictions of imperialism. If the assassin had missed, or if the Crown Prince had never been born, the war would still have taken place, on some other diplomatic pretext or other. Necessity would have expressed itself through a different "accident".

In the words of Hegel, everything which exists, exists of necessity. But, equally, everything which exists is doomed to perish, to be transformed into something else. Thus what is "necessary" in one time and place becomes "unnecessary" in another. Everything begets its opposite, which is destined to overcome and negate it. This is true of individual living things as much as societies and nature generally.

Every type of human society exists because it is necessary at the given time when it arises: "No social order ever disappears before all the productive forces for which there is room in it have been developed: and new higher relations of production never appear before the material conditions of their existence have matured in the womb of the old society. Therefore mankind always takes up only such problems as it can solve, since, looking at the matter more closely, we will always find that the problem itself arises only when the material conditions necessary for its solution already exist or at least are in the process of formation." (Marx, *Critique of Political Economy*).

Slavery, in its day, represented an enormous leap forward over barbarism. It was a necessary stage in the development of productive forces, culture and human society. As Hegel brilliantly explained it: "It is not so much from slavery as through slavery that man becomes free."

Similarly capitalism was originally a necessary and progressive stage in human society. However, like primitive communism, slavery, and feudalism, capitalism has long since ceased to represent a necessary and progressive social system. It has foundered upon the deep contradictions inherent in it, and is doomed to be overcome by the rising forces of the new society within the old, represented by the modem proletariat. Private ownership of the means of production and the nation state, the basic features of capitalist society, which originally marked a great step forward, now serve only to fetter and undermine the productive forces and threaten all the gains made in centuries of human development.

Capitalism is now a thoroughly degenerate social system, which must be overthrown and replaced by its opposite, socialism, if human culture is to survive. Marxism is determinist, but not fatalist. Men and women make history. The transformation of society can only be achieved by men and women consciously striving for their own emancipation. This struggle of the classes is not pre-determined. Who succeeds depends on many factors, and a rising, progressive class has many advantages over the old, decrepit force of reaction. But ultimately, the result must depend upon which side has the stronger will, the greater organisation and the most skilful and resolute leadership.

The victory of socialism will mark a new and qualitatively different stage of human history. To be more accurate it will mark the end of the pre-history of the human race, and start a real history.

However on the other hand, socialism marks a return to the earliest form of human society—tribal communism—but on a much higher level, which stands upon all the enormous gains of thousands of years of class society. The negation of primitive communism by class society is in turn negated by socialism. The economy of superabundance will be made possible by the application of conscious planning to the industry, science and technique established by capitalism, on a world scale. This in turn will once and for all make redundant the division of labour, the difference between mental and manual labour, between town and countryside, and the wasteful and barbaric class struggle and enable the human race at last to set its resources to the conquest of nature: to use Engels' famous phrase, "the leap of man from the realm of necessity to the realm of freedom".

Further Reading:

THE ABC OF MATERIALIST DIALECTICS
BY LEON TROTSKY

The dialectic is neither fiction nor mysticism, but a science of the forms of our thinking insofar as it is not limited to the daily problems of life but attempts to arrive at an understanding of more complicated and drawn-out processes. The dialectic and formal logic bear a relationship similar to that between higher and lower mathematics.

I will here attempt to sketch the substance of the problem in a very concise form. The Aristotelian logic of the simple syllogism starts from the proposition that "A" is equal to "A" This postulate is accepted as an axiom for a multitude of practical human actions and elementary generalisations. But in reality "A" is not equal to "A".

This is easy to prove if we observe these two letters under a lens - they are quite different from each other.

But, one can object, the question is not of the size or the form of the letters, since they are only symbols for equal quantities: for instance, a pound of sugar.

The objection is beside the point; in reality a pound of sugar is never equal to a pound of sugar—a more delicate scale always discloses a difference.

Again one can object: but a pound of sugar is equal to itself. Neither is this true—all bodies change uninterruptedly in size, weight, colour, etc. They are never equal to themselves.

A sophist will respond that a pound of sugar is equal to itself "at a given moment." Aside from the extremely dubious practical value of this "axiom," it does not withstand theoretical criticism either. How should we conceive the word 'moment'? If it is an infinitesimal interval of time, then a pound of sugar is subjected during the course of that 'moment' to inevitable changes.

Or is the "moment" a purely mathematical abstraction, that is, a zero of time? But everything exists in time; and existence itself is an uninterrupted process of transformation; time is consequently a fundamental element of existence.

Thus the axiom "A" is equal to "A" signifies that a thing is equal to itself if it does not change, that is, if it does not exist.

At first glance it could seem that these "subtleties" are useless. In reality they are of decisive significance. The axiom A is equal to A appears on one hand to be the point of departure for all our knowledge, on the other hand the point of departure for all the errors in our knowledge.

To make use of the axiom "A" is equal to "A" with impunity is possible only within certain *limits*. When quantitative changes in A are negligible for the task at hand, then we can presume "A" is equal to "A". This is, for example, the manner in which a buyer and a seller consider a pound of sugar. We consider the temperature of the sun likewise. Until recently we considered the buying power of the dollar in the same way. But quantitative changes beyond certain limits become converted into qualitative. A pound of sugar subjected to the action of water or kerosene ceases to be a pound of sugar. A dollar in the embrace of a president ceases to be a dollar. To determine at the right moment the critical point where quantity changes into quality is one of the most important and difficult tasks in all the spheres of knowledge, including sociology.

Every worker knows that it is impossible to make two completely equal objects. In the elaboration of bearing-brass into cone bearings, a certain deviation is allowed for the cones which should not, however, go beyond certain limits (this is called tolerance). By observing the norms of tolerance, the cones are considered as being equal ("A" is equal to "A"). When the tolerance is exceeded, the quantity goes over into quality; in other words, the cone bearings become inferior or completely worthless.

Our scientific thinking is only a part of our general practice, including techniques. For concepts there also exists "tolerance" which is established not by formal logic issuing from the axiom "A" is equal to "A" but by dialectical logic issuing from the axiom that everything is always changing. "Common sense" is characterized by the fact that it systematically exceeds dialectical "tolerance."

Vulgar thought operates with such concepts as capitalism, morals, freedom, workers' state, etc., as fixed abstractions, presuming that capitalism is equal to capitalism, morals are equal to morals, etc. Dialectical thinking analyses all things and phenomena in their continuous change, while determining in the material conditions of those changes that critical limit beyond which A ceases to be A, a workers' state ceases to be a workers' state.

The fundamental flaw of vulgar thought lies in the fact that it wishes to content itself with motionless imprints of reality, which consists of eternal motion. Dialectical thinking gives to concepts, by means of closer approximations, corrections, concretisations, a richness of content and flexibility, I would even say a succulence, which to a certain extent brings them close to living phenomena. Not capitalism in general but a given capitalism at a given stage of development. Not a workers' state in general, but a given workers' state in a backward country in an Imperialist encirclement, etc.

Dialectical thinking is related to vulgar thinking in the same way that a motion picture is related to a still photograph. The motion picture does not outlaw the still photograph but combines a series of them according to the laws of motion. Dialectics does not deny the syllogism, but teaches us to combine syllogisms in such a way as to bring our understanding closer to the eternally changing reality. Hegel in his *Logic* established a series of laws: change of quantity into quality, development through contradictions, conflict of content and form, interruption of continuity, change of possibility into inevitability, etc., which are just as important for theoretical thought as is the simple syllogism for more elementary tasks.

Hegel wrote before Darwin and before Marx. Thanks to the powerful impulse given to thought by the French Revolution, Hegel anticipated the general movement of science. But because it was only an *anticipation*, although by a genius, it received from Hegel an idealistic character. Hegel operated with ideological shadows as the ultimate reality. Marx demonstrated that the movement of these ideological shadows reflected nothing but the movement of material bodies.

We call our dialectic materialist since its roots are neither in heaven nor in the depths of our "free will" but in objective reality, in nature.

Consciousness grew out of the unconscious, psychology out of physiology, the organic world out of the inorganic, the solar system out of nebula. On all the rungs of this ladder of development the quantitative changes were transformed into qualitative. Our thought including dialectical thought is only one of the forms of the expression of changing matter. There is place within this system for neither God, nor Devil, nor immortal soul nor eternal norms of laws and morals. The dialectic of thinking, having grown out of the dialectic of nature, possesses consequently a thoroughly materialist character.

Darwinism, which explained the evolution of species through quantitative transformations passing into qualitative, was the highest triumph of the dialectic in the whole field of organic matter. Another great triumph was the discovery of the table of atomic weights of chemical elements and further the transformation of one element into another.

With these transformations (species, elements, etc.) is closely linked the question of classifications, just as important in the natural as in the social sciences. Linnaeus's system (eighteenth century), utilizing as its starting point the immutability of species, was limited to the description and classification of plants according to their external characteristics.

The infantile period of botany is analogous to the infantile period of logic, since the forms of our thought develop like everything that lives. Only decisive repudiation of the idea of fixed species, only the study of the history of the evolution of plants and their anatomy prepared the basis for a really scientific classification.

Marx, who in distinction from Darwin was a conscious dialectician, discovered a basis for the scientific classification of human societies in the development of their productive forces and the structure of the relations of ownership, which constitute the anatomy of society. Marxism substituted for the vulgar descriptive classification of societies and states, which even up to now still flourishes in the universities, a materialistic dialectical classification. Only through using the method of Marx is it possible correctly to determine both the concept of a workers' state and the moment of its downfall.

All this, as we see, contains nothing "metaphysical" or "scholastic," as conceited ignorance affirms. Dialectical logic expresses the laws of motion in contemporary scientific thought. The struggle against materialist dialectics on the contrary expresses a distant past conservatism of the petty bourgeoisie, the self-conceit of university routinists and . . . a spark of hope for an afterlife.

FROM 'LUDWIG FEUERBACH AND THE END OF CLASSICAL GERMAN PHILOSOPHY'
BY FREDERICK ENGELS

Out of the dissolution of the Hegelian school, however, there developed still another tendency, the only one which has borne real fruit. And this tendency is essentially connected with the name of Marx.

The separation from Hegelian philosophy was here also the result of a return to the materialist standpoint. That means it was resolved to comprehend the real world—nature and history—just as it presents itself to everyone who approaches it free from preconceived idealist crotchets. It was decided mercilessly to sacrifice every idealist which could not be brought into harmony with the facts conceived in their own and not in a fantastic interconnection. And materialism means nothing more than this. But here the materialistic world outlook was taken really seriously for the first time and was carried through consistently—at least in its basic features—in all domains of knowledge concerned.

Hegel was not simply put aside. On the contrary, a start was made from his revolutionary side, described above, from the dialectical method. But in its Hegelian form, this method was unusable. According to Hegel, dialectics is the self-development of the concept. The absolute concept does not only exist—unknown where—from eternity, it is also the actual living soul of the whole existing world. It develops into itself through all the preliminary stages which are treated at length in the Logic and which are all included in it. Then it "alienates" itself by changing into nature, where, unconscious of itself, disguised as a natural necessity, it goes through a new development and finally returns as man's consciousness of himself. This self-consciousness then elaborates itself again in history in the crude form until finally the absolute concept again comes to itself completely in the Hegelian philosophy. According to Hegel, therefore, the dialectical development apparent in nature and history—that is, the causal interconnection of the progressive movement from the lower to the higher, which asserts itself through all zigzag movements and temporary retrogression—is only a copy [*Abklatsch*] of the self-movement of the concept going on from eternity, no one knows where, but at all events independently of any thinking human brain. This ideological perversion had to be done away with. We again took a materialistic view of the thoughts in our heads, regarding them as images [*Abbilder*] of real things instead of regarding real things as images of this or that stage of the absolute concept. Thus dialectics reduced itself to the science of the general laws of motion, both of the external world and of human thought - two sets of laws which are identical in substance, but differ in their expression in so far as the human mind can apply them consciously, while in nature and also up to now for the most part in human history, these laws assert themselves unconsciously, in the form of external necessity, in the midst of an endless series of seeming accidents. Thereby the dialectic of concepts itself became merely the conscious reflex of the dialectical motion of the real world and thus the dialectic of Hegel was turned over; or rather, turned off its head, on which it was standing, and placed upon its feet. And this materialist dialectic, which for years has been our best working tool and our sharpest weapon, was, remarkably enough, discovered not only by us but also, independently of us and even of Hegel, by a German worker, Joseph Dietzgen.

In this way, however, the revolutionary side of Hegelian philosophy was again taken up and at the same time freed from the idealist trimmings which with Hegel had prevented its consistent execution. The great basic thought that the world is not to be comprehended as a complex of readymade things, but as a complex of processes, in which the things apparently stable no less than their mind images in our heads, the concepts, go through an uninterrupted change of coming into being and passing away, in which, in spite of all seeming accidentally and of all temporary retrogression, a progressive development asserts itself in the end—this great fundamental thought has, especially since the time of Hegel, so thoroughly permeated ordinary consciousness that in this generality it is now scarcely ever contradicted. But to acknowledge this fundamental thought in words and to apply it in reality in detail to each domain of investigation are two different things. If, however, investigation always proceeds from this standpoint, the demand for final solutions and eternal truths ceases once for all; one is always conscious of the necessary limitation of all acquired knowledge, of the fact that it is conditioned by the circumstances in which it was acquired. On the other hand, one no longer permits oneself to be imposed upon by the antithesis, insuperable for the still common old metaphysics, between true and false, good and bad, identical and different, necessary and accidental. One knows that these antitheses have only a relative validity; that that which is recognized now as true has also its latent false side which will later manifest itself, just as that which is now regarded as false has also its true side by virtue of which it could previously be regarded as true. One knows that what is maintained to be necessary is composed of sheer accidents and that the so-called accidental is the form behind which necessity hides itself—and so on.

The old method of investigation and thought which Hegel calls "metaphysical", which preferred to investigate things as given, as fixed and stable, a method the relics of which still strongly haunt people's minds, had a great deal of historical justification in its day. It was necessary first to examine things before it was possible to examine processes. One had first to know what a particular thing was before one could observe the changes it was undergoing. And such was the case with natural science. The old metaphysics, which accepted things as finished objects, arose from a natural science which investigated dead and living things as finished objects. But when this investigation had progressed so far that it became possible to take the decisive step forward, that is, to pass on the systematic investigation of the changes which these things undergo in nature itself, then the last hour of the old metaphysic struck in the realm of philosophy also. And in fact, while natural science up to the end of the last century was predominantly a collecting science, a science of finished things, in our century it is essentially a systematizing science, a science of the processes, of the origin and development of these things and of the interconnection which binds all these natural processes into one great whole. Physiology, which investigates the processes occurring in plant and animal organisms; embryology, which deals with the development of individual organisms from germs to maturity; geology, which investigates the gradual formation of the Earth's surface—all these are the offspring of our century.

THE THREE SOURCES AND COMPONENT PARTS OF MARXISM (EXTRACT)

BY V. I. LENIN

The philosophy of Marxism is materialism. Throughout the recent history of Europe, and particularly at the end of the eighteenth century in France, which was the scene of the decisive battle against every kind of medieval rubbish, against serfdom in institutions and ideas, materialism proved to be the only consistent philosophy, true to all the teachings of natural science, hostile to superstitions, cant, etc. The enemies of democracy tried, therefore, with all their energy, to "overthrow," undermine and defame materialism, and defended various forms of philosophic idealism, which always leads, in one way or another, to the defence and support of religion.

Marx and Engels always defended philosophic materialism in the most determined manner, and repeatedly explained the profound error of every deviation from this basis. Their views are more dearly and fully expounded in the works of Engels, *Ludwig Feuerbach* and *Anti-Duhring,* which, like the *Communist Manifesto,* are household books for every conscious worker.

However, Marx did not stop at the materialism of the eighteenth century but moved philosophy forward. He enriched it by the achievements of German classical philosophy especially by Hegel's system, which in its turn had led to the materialism of Feuerbach. Of these the main achievement is dialectics, i.e., the doctrine of development in its fuller, deeper form, free from one-sidedness-the doctrine, also, of the relativity of human knowledge that provides us with a reflection of eternally developing matter. The latest discoveries of natural science-radium, electrons, the transmutation of elements are a remarkable confirmation of the dialectical materialism of Marx, despite the doctrines of bourgeois philosophers with their "new" returns to old and rotten idealism.

While deepening and developing philosophic materialism, Marx carried it to its conclusion; he extended its perception of nature to the perception of human society. The historical materialism of Marx represented the greatest conquest of scientific thought.

Chaos and arbitrariness, which reigned until then in the views on history and politics, were replaced by a strikingly consistent and harmonious scientific theory, which shows how out of one order of social life another and higher order develops, in consequence of the growth of the productive forces—how capitalism, for instance, grows out of serfdom.

Just as the cognition of man reflects nature (i.e., developing matter) which exists independently of him, so also the social cognition of man (i.e., the various views and doctrines-philosophic, religious, political, etc.) reflects the economic order of society. Political institutions are a superstructure on the economic foundation. We see, for example, that the various political forms of modern European states serve the purpose of strengthening the domination of the bourgeoisie over the proletariat.

The philosophy of Marx completes in itself philosophic materialism which has provided humanity, and especially the working class, with a powerful instrument of knowledge.

LENIN'S COLLECTED WORKS
VOLUME 38, P359: ON THE QUESTION OF DIALECTICS

The splitting of a single whole and the cognition of its contradictory parts... is the *essence* (one of the "essentials", one of the principal, if not the principal, characteristics or features) of dialectics. That is precisely how Hegel, too, puts the matter...

The correctness of this aspect of the content of dialectics must be tested by the history of science. This aspect of dialectics (e.g. in Plekhanov) usually receives inadequate attention: the identity of opposites is taken as the sum-total of *examples* ["for example, a seed", "for example, primitive communism". The same is true of Engels. But it is "in the interests of popularisation ..."] and not as a *law of cognition* (*and* as a law of the objective world.)

In mathematics: + and -. Differential and integral.
In mechanics: action and reaction.
In physics: positive and negative electricity.
In chemistry: the combination and dissociation of atoms.
In social science: the class struggle.

The identity of opposites (it would be more correct, perhaps, to say their "unity,"—although the difference between the terms identity and unity is not particularly important here. In a certain sense both are correct) is the recognition (discovery) of the contradictory, *mutually exclusive,* opposite tendencies in *all* phenomena and processes of nature (*including* mind and society). The condition for the knowledge of all processes of the world in their *"self-movement,"* in their spontaneous development, in their real life, is the knowledge of them as a unity of opposites. Development is the "struggle" of opposites. The two basic (or two possible? Or two historically observable?) conceptions of development (evolution) are: development as decrease and increase, as repetition, *and* development as a unity of opposites (the division of a unity into mutually exclusive opposites and their reciprocal relation).

In the first conception of motion, *self*-movement, its *driving* force, its source, its motive, remains in the shade (or this source is made *external* —God, subject, etc.). In the second conception the chief attention is directed precisely to knowledge of the *source* of *"self"*-movement.

The first conception is lifeless, pale and dry. The second is living. The second *alone* furnishes the key to the "self-movement" of everything existing; it alone furnishes the key to "leaps", to the "break in continuity," to the transformation into the opposite", to the destruction of the old and the emergence of the new.

The unity (coincidence, identity, equal action) of opposites is conditional, temporary, transitory, relative. The struggle of mutually exclusive opposites is absolute, just as development and motion are absolute.

NB: The distinction between subjectivism (scepticism, sophistry, etc.) and dialectics, incidentally, is that in (objective) dialectics the difference between the relative and the absolute is itself relative. For objective dialectics there is an absolute within the relative. For subjectivism and sophistry the relative is only relative and excludes the absolute...

In his *Capital*, Marx first analyses the simplest, most ordinary and fundamental, most common and everyday *relation* of bourgeois (commodity) society, a relation encountered billions of times, viz., the exchange of commodities. In this very simple phenomenon (in this "cell" of bourgeois society) analysis reveals all the contradictions (or the germs of *all* contradictions) of modern society. The subsequent exposition shows us the development (*both* growth *and* movement) of these contradictions and of this society in the Sum of its individual parts. From its beginning to its end.

Such must also be the method of exposition (or study) of dialectics in general (for with Marx the dialectics of bourgeois society is only a particular case of dialectics). To begin with what is the simplest, most ordinary, common, etc., with any *proposition*: the leaves of a tree are green; John is a man: Fido is a dog, etc. Here already we have *dialectics* (as Hegel's genius recognised); the *individual is* the *universal*...

Consequently, the opposites (the individual is opposed to the universal) are identical: the individual exists only in the connection that leads to the universal. The universal exists only in the individual and through the individual. Every individual is (in one way or another) a universal. Every universal is (a fragment, or an aspect, or the essence of) an individual. Every universal only approximately embraces all the individual objects. Every individual enters incompletely into the universal, etc., etc. Every individual is connected by thousands of transitions with other kinds of individuals (things, phenomena, processes) etc. *Here already* we have the elements, the germs, the concepts of *necessity*, of objective connection in nature, etc. Here already we have the contingent and the necessary, the phenomenon and the essence; for when we say: John is a man, Fido is a dog, *this* is a leaf of a tree, etc., we *disregard* a number of attributes as *contingent*; we separate the essence from the appearance, and counterpose the one to the other.

Thus in *any* proposition we can (and must) disclose as in a "nucleus" ("cell") the germs of *all* the elements of dialectics, and thereby show that dialectics is a property of all human knowledge in general.

And natural science shows us (and here again it must be demonstrated in any simple instance) objective nature with the same qualities, the transformation of the individual into the universal, of the contingent into the necessary, transitions, modulations, and the reciprocal connection of opposites. Dialectics is the theory of knowledge of (Hegel and) Marxism. This is the "aspect" of the matter (it is not "an aspect" but the *essence* of the matter) to which Plekhanov, not to speak of other Marxists, paid no attention.

***

Knowledge is represented in the form of a series of circles both by Hegel (see *Logic*) and by the modern epistemologists" of natural science, the eclectic and foe of Hegelianism (which he did not understand!), Paul Volkmann.

"Circles" in philosophy: [is a chronology of *persons* - essential? No!]
Ancient: from Democritus to Plato and the dialectics of Heraclitus.
Renaissance: Descartes versus Gassendi (Spinoza?)
Modern: Holbach-Hegel (via Berkeley, Hume, Kant).
Hegel - Feuerbach - Marx

Dialectics as *living*, many-sided knowledge (with the number of sides eternally increasing), with an infinite number of shades of every approach and approximation to reality (with a philosophical system growing into a whole out of each shade)—here we have an immeasurably rich content as compared with metaphysical materialism, the fundamental *misfortune* of which is its inability to apply dialectics to the [Bildertheorie] theory of reflection, to the process and development of knowledge.

Philosophical idealism is *only* nonsense from the standpoint of crude, simple, metaphysical materialism. From the standpoint of *dialectical* materialism, on the other hand, philosophical idealism is a *one-sided*, exaggerated, development (inflation, distension) of one of the features, aspects, facets of knowledge, into an absolute, *divorced* from matter, from nature, apotheosised. Idealism is clerical obscurantism. True. But philosophical idealism is (*"more correctly"* and *"in addition"*) a *road* to clerical obscurantism *through one of the shades* of the infinitely complex *knowledge* (dialectical) of man.

Human knowledge is not (or does not follow) a straight line, but a curve, which endlessly approximates a series of circles, a spiral. Any fragment, segment, section of this curve can be transformed (transformed one-sidedly) into an independent, complete, straight line, which then (if one does not see the wood for the trees) leads into the quagmire, into clerical obscurantism (where it is anchored by the class interests of the ruling classes). Rectilinearity and one-sidedness, woodenness and petrification, subjectivism and subjective blindness—voila the epistemological roots of idealism. And clerical obscurantism (= philosophical idealism), of course, has epistemological roots, it is not groundless; it is a sterile flower undoubtedly, but a *sterile flower* that grows on the living tree of living, fertile, genuine, powerful, omnipotent, objective, absolute human knowledge.

LENIN'S COLLECTED WORKS,

VOLUME 38, pp 221-222

Summary of Dialectics

1) The determination of the concept out of itself [the thing *itself* must be considered in its relations and in its development];
2) the contradictory nature of the thing itself (the other of itself), the contradictory forces and tendencies in each phenomenon;
3) the union of analysis and synthesis.

Such apparently are the elements of dialectics.

One could perhaps present these elements in greater detail as follows:

1) the *objectivity* of consideration (not examples, not divergencies, but the Thing-in-itself).
2) the entire totality of the manifold *relations* of this thing to others.
3) the *development* of this thing, (phenomenon, respectively), its own movement, its own life.
4) the internally contradictory *tendencies* (*and* sides) in this thing.
5) the thing (phenomenon, etc) as the sum *and unity of opposites.*
6) the *struggle*, respectively unfolding, of these opposites, contradictory strivings, etc.
7) the union of analysis and synthesis—the breakdown of the separate parts and the totality, the summation of these parts.
8) the relations of each thing (phenomenon, etc.) are not only manifold, but general, universal. Each thing (phenomenon, etc.) is connected with *every other.*

9) not only the unity of opposites, but the *transitions* of *every* determination, quality, feature, side, property into *every* other [into its opposite?].
10) the endless process of the discovery of *new* sides, relations, etc.
11) the endless process of the deepening of man's knowledge of the thing, of phenomena, processes, etc., from appearance to essence and from less profound to more profound essence.
12) from co-existence to causality and from one form of connection and reciprocal dependence to another, deeper, more general form.
13) the repetition at a higher stage of certain features, properties, etc., of the lower and
14) the apparent return to the old (negation of the negation).
15) the struggle of content with form and conversely. The throwing off of the form, the transformation of the content.
16) the transition of quantity into quality and *vice versa* (15 and 16 are *examples* of 9)

In brief, dialectics can be defined as the doctrine of the unity of opposites. This embodies the essence of dialectics, but it requires explanations and development.

***

Questions on Dialectical Materialism

1) Why does the working class need a philosophy?
2) Is "common sense" a philosophy?
3) What is materialism?
4) What is idealism?
5) Is Darwin's theory of evolution correct?
6) What is meant by metaphysical?
7) How would you define dialectics?
8) What was wrong with the old materialism?
9) What is formal logic?
10) Does a pound of sugar equal a pound of sugar?
11) Why do workers sometimes accept major attacks on their terms and conditions, then strike over a tea break, washing up time or other "small" incident?
12) Does history repeat itself?
13) Was the First World War caused by the assassination of a Crown Prince in Sarajevo? What is the role of accident in history?
14) Can you be in one place and another at the same time?

15) What was Hegel's great contribution to philosophy?
16) What was the contribution of Marx and Engels to philosophy?
17) Why can it be said that nature is the proof of dialectics?
18) What is the relevance of dialectical materialism in understanding the future?
19) Did the the universe have a beginning?
20) Why are Marxists determinists?

Suggested Reading List

The Poverty of Philosophy, Marx
Economic and Philosophical Manuscripts, Marx
Ludwig Feuerbach and the end of classical German Philosophy, Engels
The German Ideology (Student edition), Marx and Engels
Anti-Duhring, Engels (out of print)
Dialectics of Nature, Engels
(Both the above are in the *M&E Collected Works*, vol 25),
Socialism Utopian and Scientific, Engels
Materialism and Empirio-Criticism (Collected Works, vol 17), Lenin
Philosophical Notebooks (Collected Works, volume 38), Lenin
On Marx and Engels, Lenin
The Three Sources and Component Parts of Marxism, Lenin
Introduction to the Logic of Marxism, Novack
Reason in Revolt - Marxist Philosophy and modern science, Woods and Grant
The Fundamental Problems of Marxism, Plekhanov (out of print)
The Development of the Monist View of History, Plekhanov (out of print)
In Defence of Marxism, Trotsky
Radio, Science, Technology and Society, Trotsky (out of print)
The Logic, Hegel (out of print)
Historical articles at marxist.com

Obtainable from Wellred Books, PO Box 50525, London E14 6WG
Or at the online Marxist bookshop at wellred.marxist.com
An important Marxist online resouce is at marxists.org

Historical Materialism

By Mick Brooks

Historical Materialism is the application of Marxist science to historical development. The fundamental proposition of historical materialism can be summed up in a sentence: ""it is not the consciousness of men that determines their existence, but, on the contrary, their social existence that determines their consciousness." (Marx, in *The Preface to* A *Contribution to the Critique of Political Economy.)*

What does this mean?

Readers of the *Daily Mirror* will be familiar with the "Perishers" cartoon strip. In one incident the old dog, Wellington wanders down to a pool full of crabs. The crabs speculate about the mysterious divinity, the "eyeballs in the sky," which appears to them.

The point is, that is actually how you would look at things if your universe were a pond. Your consciousness is determined by your being. Thought is limited by the range of experience of the species.

We know very little about how primitive people thought, but we know what they couldn't have been thinking about. They wouldn't have wandered about wondering what the football results were, for instance. League football presupposes big towns able to get crowds large enough to pay professional footballers and the rest of the club staff. Industrial towns in their turn can only emerge when the productivity of labour has developed to the point where a part of society can be fed by the rest, and devote themselves to producing other requirements than food.

In other words, an extensive division of labour must exist. The other side of this is that people must be accustomed to working for money and buying the things they want from others-including tickets to the football-which of course was not the case in primitive society.

So this simple example shows how even things like professional football are dependent on the way society makes its daily bread, on people's "social existence".

After all, what is mankind? The great *idealist* philosopher Hegel said that "man, is a *thinking being."* Actually Hegel's view was a slightly more sophisticated form of the usual religious view that man is endowed by his Creator with a brain to admire His handiwork.

It is true that thinking *is* one way we are different from dung beetles, sticklebacks and lizards. But why did humans develop the capacity to think?

Over a hundred years ago, Engels pointed out that upright posture marked the transition from ape to man, a completely materialist explanation. This view has been confirmed by the most recent researches of anthropologists such as Leakey.

Upright posture liberated the hands for gripping with an opposable thumb. This enabled tools to be used and developed.

Upright posture also allowed early humans to rely more on the eyes, rather than the other senses, for sensing the world around. The use of the hands developed the powers of the brain through the medium of the eyes.

Engels was a dialectical materialist. In no way did he minimise the importance of thought-rather he *explained* how it arose. We can also see that Benjamin Franklin, the eighteenth-century US politician and inventor, was much nearer a materialist approach than Hegel when he defined man as a *tool-making animal.*

Darwin showed a hundred years ago that there is a struggle for existence, and species survive through natural selection. At first sight early humans didn't have a lot going for them, compared with the speed of the cheetah, the strength of the lion, or the sheer intimidating bulk of the elephant. Yet humans came to dominate the planet and, more recently, to drive many of these more fearsome animals to the point of extinction.

What differentiates mankind from the lower animals is that, however self-reliant animals such as lions may seem, they ultimately just take external nature around them for granted, whereas, mankind progressively masters nature.

The process whereby mankind masters nature is *labour.* At Marx's grave, Engels stated that his friend's great discovery was that "mankind must first of all eat, drink, have shelter and clothing, and therefore work before it can pursue politics, science, art, religion etc.

In another dialectical formulation, Engels says that "the hand is not only the organ of labour, it is also the product of labour."

While we can't read the minds of our primitive human beings, we can make a pretty good guess about what they were thinking most of the time—food. The struggle against want has dominated history ever since.

Marxists are often accused of being *'economic determinists'.* Actually, Marxists are far from denying the importance of ideas or the active role of individuals in history. But precisely because we are active, we understand the *limits* of individual activity, and the fact that the appropriate social conditions must exist before our ideas and our activity can be effective.

Our academic opponents are generally passive cynics who exalt individual activity amid the port and walnuts from over-stuffed armchairs. We understand, with Marx that people "make their own history...but under circumstances directly encountered, given and transmitted from the past". We need to understand how society is developing in order to intervene in the process. That is what we mean when we say Marxism is a science of perspectives.

Language, the currency of thought, is itself the creation of labour. We can see this even among jackals and other hunting animals that rely upon teamwork rather than just brute force or speed to kill their prey. They have a series of barked commands and warnings—the beginnings of language.

That is how language evolved among people, as a result of their co-operative labour. The germs of rational thinking among the higher apes, and the limited use of tools by some animals, have remained at a beginning stage, while reaching fruition only in human beings.

We have seen that labour distinguishes mankind from the other animals—that mankind progressively changes nature through labour, and in doing so changes itself. It follows that there is a real measure of progress through all the miseries and pitfalls of human history—the increasing ability of men and women to master nature and subjugate it to their own requirements: in other words, the increasing *productivity of labour.*

To each stage in the development of the productive forces corresponds a certain set of *production relations.*

Production relation means the way people organise themselves to gain their daily bread. Production relations are thus the skeleton of every form of society. They provide the conditions of social existence that determine human consciousness.

Marx explained how the development of the productive forces brings into existence different production relations, and different forms of class society.

By a 'class' we mean a group of people in society with the same relationship to the means of production. The class which owns and controls the means of production rules society. This, at the same time, enables it to force the oppressed or labouring class to toil in the rulers' interests. The labouring class is forced to produce a surplus which the ruling class lives off.

Marx explained:

"The specific economic form in which unpaid *surplus-labour is* pumped out of the direct producers determines the relationship of rulers and ruled, as it grows directly out of production itself and, in turn, reacts upon it as a determining element. Upon this, however, is founded the entire formation of the economic community which grows up out of the production relations themselves; thereby simultaneously its specific political form. It is always the direct relationship of the owners of the conditions of production to the direct producers-a relation always naturally corresponding to a definite stage in the development of the methods of labour and thereby its social productivity-which reveals the innermost secret, the hidden basis of the entire social structure, and with it the political form of the relation of sovereignty and dependence, in short the corresponding specific form of the state. *(Capital,* Vol III.)

Primitive Communism

In the earliest stages of society people did not go into factories, work to produce things they would not normally consume, and be 'rewarded' at the end of the week with pieces of coloured paper or decorated discs which other people would be quite prepared to accept in exchange for the food, clothing, etc., which they needed. Such behaviour would have struck our remote ancestors as quite fantastic.

Nor did many of the other features of modern society we so much take for granted exist. What socialist has not heard the argument "People are bound to be greedy and grabbing. You can't get socialism because you can't change human nature?

In fact, society *divided into classes* has existed for no more than about 10,000 years-one hundredth of the time mankind has been on this planet. For the other 99% of the time there was no class society, that is, no enforced inequalities, no state, and no family in the modern sense.

This was not because primitive people were unaccountably more noble than us, but because production relations produced a different sort of society, and so a different 'human nature'. Being determines consciousness, and if people's social being changes—if the society they live under changes—then their consciousness will also change.

The basis of primitive society was gathering and hunting. The only division of labour was that between men and women for the entirely natural biological reason that women were burdened much of the time with young children. They gathered vegetable foods while the men hunted.

Thus each sex played an important part in production. On the basis of studying tribes such as the !Kung in the Kalahari desert, who still live under primitive communist conditions, it has been estimated that the female contribution to the food supply may well have been more important than the male's.

All these tribal societies had features in common. The hunting grounds were regarded as the common property of the tribe. How could they be anything else when hunting itself is a collective activity? The very insecurity of existence leads to sharing. It's no good hiding a dead hippo from your mates—you won't be able to eat it before it rots anyway, and there may well come a time when other tribesmen have a superfluity while you're in distress. It's common sense to share and share alike.

Private property did exist in personal implements, but in the most different tribal societies there existed similar rules to burn or bury these with the body of the owner, in order to prevent the accumulation of inequality. Even after these tribes began to develop agriculture there was a progressive redivision of the land, so strong were the norms of primitive communism. The Roman historian Tacitus noted such rules among the German tribes.

Women were held in high esteem in such societies. They contributed at least equally to the wealth of the tribe. They developed separate skills—it seems women invented pottery and even made the crucial breakthrough to agriculture.

No such institution as *the state* was necessary, for there were no fundamental antagonistic class interests tearing society apart. Individual disputes could be sorted out within the tribe.

Old men with experience certainly played leading parts in the decision-making of the tribe. They were chiefs, however, and not kings—their authority was deserved or it did not exist. As late as the third century AD (when it was ceasing to be true) Athanaric, leader of the German tribe, the Visigoths, said: "I have authority, not power".

Society developed because it had to. Beginning in tropical Africa, as population grew to cover more inhospitable parts of the globe, people had to use their power of thought and labour to develop—or die. From gathering fruit, nuts, etc., it was a step forward to cultivating the land—actually ensuring that vegetable food was to hand. From hunting it was a step to husbandry, penning in the animals. Tribal society remained the norm.

The first great revolution in mankind's history was the agricultural, or neolithic revolution. Grains were selected and sown, and the ground ploughed up with draught animals. For the first time a substantial *surplus* over and above the subsistence needs of the toilers came into existence.

Under primitive communism there had been simply no basis for an idle class. There was no point in enslaving someone else, since they could only provide for their own needs. Now the possibility arose for idleness for *some,* but mankind could still not provide enough for *everyone* to lead such a life.

On this basis, *class societies* arose—societies divided between possessing and labouring classes.

The main issue in the class struggle down the ages has been the struggle over the surplus produced by the toilers. The way this surplus was appropriated—grabbed—depended on the different mode of production inaugurated by agriculture. This change provided the base for the complete transformation of social life.

Tribal norms died hard. At first, land was redivided. Even in feudal Europe, village communities in some areas carried on the traditions of primitive communism in a transmuted form by redivision of the original peasant land.

But agriculture, unlike hunting, could be more an individual activity. By working harder you could get more and, when everyone lived on the margin of survival, that was important.

Moreover, the agricultural revolution—involving the use of draught animals in ploughing, etc., mainly handled by men—relegated women to the home, working up materials provided by the man. It was the lack of a direct role in production that led to the world—historic defeat of the female sex.

Men wanted to pass on their unequal property to a male heir. In primitive communist society *descent* had been traced through the female line *(inheritance* had been unimportant). Now inheritance began to be traced through the male line.

We do not know exactly how class society came into being, but we can piece together the story from bits of evidence available to us. We call this process a revolution, and so it was in the profoundest sense of the word.

But we must remember that transitional forms between the different types of society were in existence for hundreds, perhaps thousands, of years before the new type definitively replaced the old. Human progress did not proceed evenly but according to the *law of combined and uneven development.*

It was not the well-situated people of equatorial Africa, but people in more temperate climes (probably the near East) who were first forced to develop agriculture.

The first agriculture was of course very rudimentary, probably consisting of 'slash and burn' cultivation. This meant that the tribe kept on the move, for the cleared land offered good crops for only a couple of years before yields dropped off.

Thus tribal society remained in existence, but underwent modifications. Tacitus describes the military democracy of the German tribes of his time, with a constitution of a war chief, councils of elders and assembly of warriors (women had now been disenfranchised). This was typical for tribes at this stage of development.

Though the assembly could reject or approve all decisions (by banging their spears on their shields), in the war chief we see the embryo of a king, and in the council of elders the outline of a ruling aristocracy.

The landlord rulers of Rome were organised in the senate ("old men") and the Anglo-Saxon kings were advised by a Witan ("'wise men"), both relics of a democratic tribal constitution that had been turned into its opposite. The German tribes were now organised for warfare *because a surplus existed,* however precariously, which could be taken unless defended.

Anthropologists such as Leakey have shown that, contrary to the views of writers such as Desmond Morris *(The Naked Ape)* and Robert Ardrey *(The Hunting Hypothesis),* the human being is not *inherently* aggressive. While primitive communist societies engaged in battles, e.g. over scarce hunting grounds, wars began to be an *established and regular feature* of history *only* at the stage when there was something worth fighting for.

We have spoken of agriculture as being the breakthrough to a society where a surplus could be produced. In fact the raising of the productivity of labour made possible by agriculture allowed a more extensive division of labour—people could turn their hands to producing other things.

So the agricultural revolution brought in its train associated revolutions in technique (such as in pottery and metal-working) and in the whole social structure.

Inequalities developed between different tribal peoples as well as within the tribes. For geographical and other reasons some tribes began to concentrate on stock rearing, fishing, etc.

As agricultural peoples began to settle down around villages fortified to protect their surplus (or rather, the surplus some of their number had acquired) these fishing and stock-rearing peoples took over the job of exchanging goods. Before, exchange had been a casual act between tribes who met one another on their travels. Now it became a regular occasion.

Metal was of course one of the most important items of trade. The Jews were one of the most famous stock-rearing peoples (in the Bible, the wealth of Abraham is always measured in herds) who developed into traders between Egypt and the Mediterranean civilisations.

Trade developed from ritual gifts between tribes. What was the measure of the value of a gift? As soon as people could form some conception of how long it took to produce the gifts they got, they would attempt to outdo the donors in generosity by giving the product of more labour in return.

As trade became more regular, the need naturally arose for a *universal* equivalent—something which could readily be exchanged in trade and which would be accepted generally as a measure of value. At first this need was met by cattle (the Latin *pecunia* meaning 'money' is derived from *pecus* meaning cattle).

Later this need was fulfilled more conveniently by ingots of metal, in which there was a burgeoning trade, and which were stamped by the monarchs as a guarantee of weight.

Ritual gifts would usually be given to the chief as representative of the tribe. As society grew wealthier, it became worth-while to be a chief. The chief's house became the beginnings of a market place in the village.

Metal working placed a tremendous new power for good or ill in the hands of men. Metal, particularly copper and bronze, was rare. The first need of these new societies was defence of the living standards they had built up. Naturally the tribal chief, as the leading fighting man should be first to avail himself of the new strategic material.

The consequences of this are to be seen in the legends of the ancient Greek poet, Homer. He describes the city of Troy beseiged by an army of bronze-armoured Greek military aristocrats. Not mentioned much are the host of common soldiers, often armed only with flint-tipped spears, who did most of the fighting and dying. Clearly they are not considered a subject for literature.

The ancient legends of Homer depict a society where primitive communism had been thrust aside by the evolution of tribal chiefs through a life of war and plunder into a network of aristocrats and kings. A ruling class now had the monopoly of effective, armed, might. Thus the development of tribal society had-produced its own 'grave-diggers', putting an end to classless equality.

Incidentally, the Germanic sagas arose at an identical stage in the dissolution of German tribal society. Their "heroic age, produced similar art forms (epic poetry) and even a similar system of the gods, corresponding to a similar stage in the development of production as in ancient Greece.

The Bronze Age civilisation described by Homer was swept away by Dorian invasions, a period equivalent to the west-European Dark Ages. The historical record dies out for hundreds of years. But the invaders brought something new—iron.

Iron was potentially more plentiful than bronze. Homer's ruling class could not have used it to arm the common people, for that would have deprived them of their military monopoly, the basis of their social power. They fell before invaders who were still tribesmen.

The invaders' society was not class-divided. So they all used iron weapons and were invincible for their time. Sometimes mankind has to step back in order to go forward.

The Asiatic Mode of Production

Civilisation developed differently in different places. So far as we know, it arose first in the Nile delta of Egypt and in Mesopotamia (in what is now Iraq), though recent discoveries suggest it may also have developed independently in India and in South-East Asia at around the same time.

In both Egypt and Mesopotamia the ruling class seems to have sprung from the elevation of a stratum of priests, rather than chiefs, above the rest of society. This is because the priests had the leisure to develop a calendar, allowing them to foretell the coming of the Nile floods, and arithmetic to develop the centrally planned irrigation works which first produced a massive surplus.

The interest of Egyptian priests in maths and astronomy was thus not accidental, but rooted in the requirements of production.

Because of the requirements of planned irrigation, as Marx explains: "The communal conditions for real appropriation through labour, such as irrigation systems (very important among the Asian peoples), means of communication, etc., will then appear as the work of the superior entity—the despotic government which is poised above the small communities."

The Asiatic state which was not accountable in any way to the village communities, will feel entitled to appropriate the surplus as a tribute. This tribute is exacted through state ownership of the land: "...the integrating entity which stands above all these small communities may appear as the superior or sole proprietor, and the real communities therefore only as hereditary possessors."

The villages were largely self-sufficient, rendering tribute to the Asiatic despotism in order for the "general conditions of production " (irrigation, etc.) to be maintained. Handicrafts and agriculture were combined within each village. The dispersed villages were unable to organise effectively against their exploitation, so the whole system was very resistant to change.

This is what Marx and Engels meant when they said that such societies were "'outside history". India, for instance, was invaded by one set of conquerors after another, but none of these political changes reached beneath the surface.

The Ptolemies, Greek successors of Alexander the Great, who came from a society where private property in land was at the root of their social system, left the system as they found it when they conquered Egypt. After all they were very satisfied with the revenues it provided them.

It was only after thousands of years, when British capitalism conquered India and strove to introduce private property in land in order to destroy the unity of native agriculture and handicrafts, and develop the preconditions for capitalism, that the Asiatic mode of production was finally destroyed. The result was the decline of the irrigation systems and a series of horrible famines throughout the nineteenth century.

The Asiatic mode of production saw the first development of class society, though retaining certain features of primitive communism, such as collective tilling of the soil. It raised production to a higher level than it had ever been before, and then stagnated.

Thus, in vast areas of the globe, there arose a form of society completely different from anything seen in Western Europe. Slavery was known, but it was not the dominant mode of production. In contrast with western feudalism, the surplus was extorted by the central state rather than by landlords.

Once civilisation was established and maintained, it was bound to radiate its effects all around it, whether through war or trade. Egypt was always dependent on outside areas for trade, thus stimulating the advance of civilisation in Crete and thereby giving an enormous impetus to the trading communities on the Greek coast to develop. Here civilisation found relations of production—private land-ownership providing an unlimited spur to private enrichment—which could take humanity forward again.

Ancient Greece: Slavery and Democracy

Thus, when Greece next enters the historical record, its class structure is very different from the time of Homer. Trading cities have sprung up all around the coast. All these cities seem to have been dominated at first by small ruling classes of landlords who monopolised political rights.

We can speculate that these landlords may have been the original occupants of the central city zones. As trade developed, the price of their land would have rocketed, and they would have been able to use their position to control the marketing of produce. Certainly they used their dominant position to lend seed to the poorer citizens living on the outskirts, and to enforce a debt bondage on many. (It is still a matter of scholarly debate whether the rural people mortgaged their lands or themselves but the form of exploitation is not important for us here).

As trade developed, the merchant and artisan classes grew in importance, and campaigned with the poor peasants for political rights. Once class society had been established, it radiated throughout the main population centres through warfare and the chance of getting yourself a slice of the surplus.

All city states in Greece and Rome were organised around the same principles. The whole city-state ('polis' in Greek) was unified against every other city-state, but divided within itself.

It was divided on *class* lines—and between *citizens* and *slaves.*

At first the poor citizens ('plebeians' as they were called in Rome) were blocked from all political rights. Their struggle was political—to gain a say in the decision making of the state.

Military survival was also a necessity, and for that the state depended on the support of the peasantry in the army. The wealthy landlord class needed the poor citizens to fight for them. That is why a representative of the upper class, Solon in Athens (the case we know best), actually redistributed the land to the plebeians in 594 B.C.

In Athens, a predominantly trading centre with a higher concentration of merchants and artisans, the small men were eventually able to win full democratic rights. Poor men were paid for public service, and over 5,000 citizens regularly met in the assembly to discuss policy.

The struggle for democracy went through a number of stages. In city after city the landed oligarchy were first overthrown by tyrants. These men bore a remarkable resemblance to the later absolutist monarchs who balanced between the feudal aristocracy and the rising class of merchant capitalists.

Like the absolutists, they used the deadlock in the class struggle to grab political power for themselves. Like the Tudor monarchs in England, the political stability they guaranteed allowed the further rise of the monied classes, who from being their sturdiest prop became their staunchest foe, as they themselves formed aspirations to untrammelled political power. So the era of the tyrants ended in all the commercial cities of Greece in 'democratic' revolution.

But Athenian democracy—democracy for the *citizens*—had as its foundation *the exploitation of a class of non-citizens: slaves who were without political rights.* Athenian democracy was in fact a mechanism for enforcing the interests of the ruling class over the exploited slave class—and for defending the interests of the ruling class in war.

The *polis* was an institution geared up for permanent war. The power of the city state was based on independent peasants capable of arming themselves ('hoplites'). The victory of democracy was inevitable in Athens after the poor citizens won the naval battle of Salamis against the Persians for the city. Though too poor to arm themselves, they provided the rowers for the Athenian navy. A precarious unity of interests was established between rich and poor citizens through expansion outwards and the conquest of slaves.

By comparison with later Roman slave society the Greek slave mode of production was relatively "democratic"—as far as *the citizens were concerned.* Even poor citizens could own a slave to help around the farm or workshop, or lease them out to work on slave gangs.

Thus the squeeze was off the poor citizen, for the rich had an alternative labour supply. The Greek states where democracy did not develop were mainly inland, where landed wealth was naturally more important than commercial riches.

Slavery itself was only possible because labour was now capable of yielding a surplus. That surplus was appropriated by a ruling class who owned the means of production—in this case the slaves themselves. The state was the state of the ruling class. The whole structure of society was based upon slave labour—all the miracles of art, culture and philosophy were only possible because an exploited class laboured so slave-holders could have leisure.

Slave society had its own dynamic. Its success depended upon the continual appropriation of more slaves, more unpaid labour.

"Wherever *slavery is* the main form of production it turns labour into servile activity, consequently makes it dishonourable for freemen. Thus the way out of such a mode of production is barred, while on the other hand slavery is an impediment to more developed production, which urgently requires its removal. This contradiction spells the doom of all production based on slavery and of all communities based on it. A solution comes about in most cases through the forcible subjection of the deteriorating communities by other, stronger ones (Greece by Macedonia and later Rome). As long as these themselves have slavery as their foundation there is merely a shifting of the centre and a repetition of the process on a higher plane until (Rome) finally a people conquers that replaces slavery by another form of production." (Engels, in his preparatory writings for *Anti-Duhring).*

To illustrate this explanation, let us turn to Rome, where slavery exhausted its potential, and Western European society finally blundered out of the blind alley it found itself in.

Roman Slavery

Roman society, after the expulsion of its early kings, presents at first the same aspect as the Greek city states when they were dominated by landlords (in Rome called "patricians" and organised in the Senate).

Initially they monopolised all political rights. The plebeians waged a magnificent struggle for a share in power, including the use of the agrarian general strike, in the form of a 'secession of the tribes'.

But the plebeians were not just poor citizens. They included wealthy merchants who just wanted to join the patricians in their control of state power. They headed the plebeian movement and, when they got what they wanted out of it, deserted it. One of the definite gains of. these struggles was the abolition of debt bondage. The gap was filled by the massive expansion of the Roman republic and, through conquest, the acquisition of hordes of slaves.

The difference with Greece was that the Roman patricians hung on to power, despite the concessions wrung from them, and monopolised the benefits of this influx. They linked slave labour to the explotation of the great farms *(latifundia)*. In so doing they inevitably undercut the plebians who, organised in legions, provided the basis for Roman military greatness.

The dispossessed legionaires could come back after twenty years of military service to find their farms choked with weeds. Inevitably they were ruined and drifted into the town to form a rootless, propertyless proletariat. But as the nineteenth century anti-capitalist social critic Sismondi said, "whereas the Roman proletariat lived at the expense of society, modern society lives at the expense of the proletariat".

In Rome the Gracchus brothers led a last desperate struggle to save the independent plebeians. Both were cut down by the bought mob of the patricians.

The crisis of Roman society in the first century B.C.,the last century of the republic, was two-fold in origin.

On the one hand the class struggle had reached a deadlock. The contradictions spilled over into the army. One general after another cemented the support of their troops to their own political ambitions by promising grants of land which the plebeians could not get through their own struggle.

On the other hand, a tiny oligarchy from Rome was now ruling a world empire through corrupt provincial governors and tax collectors. This form of rule was quite inadequate. This was brought home in the Social Wars, when Rome's Italian allies rose in revolt for rights of citizenship. The only way the Romans could 'win' was by enlisting Italian allies on their side—by offering rights of citizenship!

So one military man after another stepped into the power vacuum and progressively enlarged their own power. Finally Caesar Augustus did away with the republic, relying particularly on the Italian landlords, whom he gave a say in the running of the state.

Gradually all became citizens, and the privilege was made meaningless, for all were mere subjects of the Roman Empire. Not for nothing did critics of the French emperor, Napoleon Bonaparte, call his policies 'Caesarism'. Exactly the same balancing between classes and groups while building up personal power characterised both men. Augustus' empire inaugurated a long period of peace. But for a slave empire, peace is more a menace than war. The supply of slaves dried up and the price of slaves rose disastrously. Rome had reached its natural frontiers. It was surrounded by tribes, known as "barbarians", which it could not conquer.

Decline of the Roman Empire

In this situation the limits of slave production showed themselves. The slave has no incentive to develop production. He only works under threat of the whip. Free men for their part despised labour, which they associated with being an *"instrumentum vocale"*, an 'item of property with a voice', as the Roman jurists called slaves.

The tragedy of Roman society was that the class struggle was three-cornered. The poor freemen had their quarrel with the great slave-holders, but the only pathetic bit of dignity they had to hang on to was that they were free men, and thus they always made common cause with their oppressors in the army of the polls in conquering lands for slaves and holding down slave rebellions.

The slaves for their part lived in a world where slavery was universal, and so dreamed for the most part of "'enslaving the slave-holders", not creating a world without slaves.

The burden of keeping together this enormous empire created a huge swollen state power which guzzled up a great part of the surplus in taxes. The only self-confident force capable of acting in a centralised way among the human atoms created by imperial despotism was the army. For a hundred years the praetorian guard made and unmade emperors at their pleasure.

The emperors had one way out of this—to withdraw legions from the frontier and march against the praetorian guard in Rome. All this did was to reproduce the contradictions on a bigger scale.

When the Emperor Septimus Severus died, he offered this piece of distilled political wisdom to his sons: "Pay the soldiers. Nothing else matters." Nobody in the Roman empire made any secret of the fact that the state is essentially "armed bodies of men".

As productivity declined, so naturally did trade, and the villas of the land-owners became increasingly self-sufficient, developing in the direction of the medieval manor which was to replace them. The flight from money was further boosted by inflation at the end of the third century. The emperors made sure that they didn't lose out, by demanding taxes in kind.

At the same time they were squeezing the patrician (landlord) class, now deprived of political power, by forcing them to shell out enormous amounts on building and circuses. The landlords responded by fleeing to the country and setting up on their self-sufficient country estates.

Slavery was beginning to die out, not because of humanitarian ideas supposedly introduced by Christianity, but because it simply did not pay. The only way slave production could take society forward was through the conquest of enormous numbers of slaves who could be worked to death in a few years and replaced.

These conquests had been made possible by the Roman legions of armed plebeians. But the plebeians had been destroyed by the very success of big slave-worked farms.

By this time the Romans could only find barbarian mercenaries to man their armies. Thus Rome was defended from the barbarians by barbarians! Clearly the empire was living on borrowed time.

Slavery was still important, particularly in domestic service to the rich, but it gradually ceased to be the dominant mode of production. As production and trade shrank, it became clear to the landlords that it was pointless feeding men to work on the fields all the year round when, because of the natural rhythms of agricultural work, they were idle half the time. Much better to get them to fend for themselves in periods of slack!

Former slaves were rented plots of land from which they had to pay a regular part of their produce to the landlord as well as wrench a subsistence for their family. The state also derived most of its revenue from a land tax which pressed on the peasantry.

In time, because of the natural tendency for peasants to get into debt in times of bad harvest, they were bound to the soil in a serf-like condition. This is called the period of the "colonate".

Eventually the Western Empire was overthrown, not because the barbarians had become more aggressive and threatening, but because of the inner rottenness of the empire. We have seen that the productive forces were already in decline; and in the colonate some of the tendencies, that were to come to fruition under feudalism, were in the process of coming into existence.

The Transition to Feudalism

The new society created after the Germanic (barbarian) invasions of Western Europe was a synthesis of declining Roman civilisation and German tribal society in the process of evolving into class society.

Like the Dorian invasion of early Greek civilisation it seemed a step back. The decline in production affected every area of social life. Such chronicles of the Dark Ages as survived (like Gregory of Tours' *History of the Franks)* show a childlike credulity in all kinds of ridiculous miracles—an attitude which would have been laughed to scorn by a Roman patrician historian.

All the achievements of art and culture only survived in suspended animation in the institutions of the church. But the barbarians also brought new ideas and a possibility of moving forward once again. To take just one example, the Germans had developed a heavy plough which turned over a furrow rather than just scratching at the surface, and so increased grain yields.

What had been happening among the German tribes in the meantime? The Romans had maintained themselves for an amazing period of time by 'dividing in order to rule'. They didn't just divide tribe against tribe, but consciously developed trade of luxuries to rear a privileged elite among the tribes who were bought off, and so divided each tribe against itself.

As early as the first century A.D., Tacitus, after describing the democratic constitution of most of the tribes, moves on to the Suiones, a sea trading people:

"Wealth, too, is held in high honour; and so a single monarch rules with no restrictions on his power and with an unquestioned claim to obedience. Arms are not, as in the rest of Germany, allowed to all and sundry, but are kept in charge of a custodian who in fact is a slave...idle crowds of armed men easily get into mischief."

Since tribal society had no state, there was no possibility of preventing the young men from going out on raiding parties. We all know from cowboy films- the problems the old chief of the Apaches has in explaining this principle to the Colonel of the Seventh Cavalry. But whereas the Indian resistance to capitalist conquest was doomed, raiding parties into the declining Roman empire could do very well for themselves.

Retinues built up around the boldest young men. These armed retinues were thus dependent on an individual and not on the will of the tribe. They were attached to their leader by gifts of booty. They were the beginning of the end for tribal society, for bit by bit they became a permanent armed aristocracy, and elevated their leader to king.

This military aristocracy expropriated the Roman landlords or merged with them as they entered the territory of the Roman empire.

It is not the purpose of this pamphlet to trace all the detailed shifts West European society went through in the next few centuries. But it is instructive to look at the most serious attempt to replace the lost lustre of the centralised Roman empire, the Frankish empire of Charlemagne, and what happened to it.

Charlemagne conquered huge areas of Europe and set up provinces governed by counts. To provide food for the armies carrying out his conquests, the formerly free Frankish peasantry ("Frank", means free) were increasingly reduced to serf status.

These endeavours were greater than the productive resources of society could bear. Because productivity was low, communications were primitive. Under Charlemagne's successors the empire imploded, invaded by Normans, Vikings, and Saracens, and seemed on the point of collapse.

The local magnates seized their opportunity, setting up castles everywhere and becoming undisputed lords of the local villages, in return for defence of the land.

Charlemagne's successors had to accept the situation, granting land instead of gifts and accomodation to their men at arms, and demanding acknowledgement of sovereignty and military service in return. It was a measure of the stage society was at that land was the main form of wealth—command over land gave access to the privileges of the surplus.

Feudal Society

Feudal society thus emerged in the form of a pyramid of military obligations to those above in exchange for command of the land to those below.

The whole structure relied on the unpaid labour of the peasants working on the lords' land. Unlike slaves, they were not the property of the lord. Feudalism developed untidily. Some in the village were in possession of very little land and either existed still as slaves or as household servants working on the lord's land. Freer peasants had land to till and had to pay a rent in kind. Others had an intermediate status, working small plots to gain their own subsistence and forced to pay labour services the rest of the time, on the lord's land.

Exploitation under feudalism is clear and unveiled. The peasants pay services in money, labour or produce to the lords. Everyone can see what is going on. If the lord is in a position to force the peasant to work four days instead of three on his land, then it is clear to both parties that the rate of exploitation has been increased.

Under slavery, on the contrary, even the part of the working week which the slave has to work to gain his own subsistence seems to be unpaid. He therefore seems to work for nothing. Under capitalism, the wage worker is paid a sum of money which is presented as being the value of his labour. All labour seems to be paid.

In all three systems the producer is exploited: but the particular form of exploitation ultimately determined the whole structure of society.

Under feudalism the 'bodies of armed men' which comprised the state were mainly drawn from the ruling class, who had a monopoly of armed might. So political and economic power were in the same hands.

Justice in the village was largely in the hands of the lords' manorial courts. The feudal lord and his men-at-arms were police, judge, and executioners all rolled into one.

Looking back, we tend to regard feudalism as a static system. Compared to capitalism it undoubtedly was. But substantial advances were made under the stabilisation that feudalism provided.

For instance, the population of England probably doubled between 1066 and the fourteenth century—a mark of the advances in production. Large areas of forest and uncultivated land were put under plough for the first time. Huge regions of Eastern Europe were colonised by feudalism.

Feudalism provided a limited incentive for the producer to expand production for his own advantage. Sometimes the lord took the lead in developing agriculture or colonisation, sometimes the peasants. This depended on the class struggle. The tendency was for the lord to try to reduce the peasants' plots to a minimum, encroach on the common lands, and impose serf status. The peasants, on the other hand, were interested in reducing feudal dues to a minimum rent.

Innovations such as water and wind-mills were introduced under the new system. The lord would attempt to appropriate all the benefits of this advance by charging exorbitant fees for time use of his mill.

On the continent of Europe in the later middle ages, these 'banalities' were the main form of feudal revenue. Whether the incentive to produce more came from the lord's desire for more revenue for luxuries, or from the ambition of the peasants to set themselves up in business as independent farmers, production crept up.

But feudalism, like slavery before it imposed limits on the development of productivity. From generation to generation agricultural productivity was largely stagnant. The easiest way for the feudal lords to gain more wealth was to exploit more people. There was therefore a perpetual impulse to warfare, the net effect of which was to waste and destroy the productive forces.

Medieval Towns

Like previous forms of class society, feudalism in its development produced the germs of a new society in the towns.

Roman towns had been much bigger and more impressive than the towns of the feudal middle ages, but they did not have the same possibilities for development. Roman cities started out as collections of landlords with an attendant trade in luxuries, and as administrative centres which fleeced the surrounding countryside. Medieval cities, on the other hand, were centres of trade and handicrafts.

As productivity developed, trade necessarily grew. Artisans, who had been attached to aristocratic households and monasteries in the dark ages, gathered together to trade with the rural areas in goods that could be produced quicker and therefore cheaper, or could only be produced by skilled specialists.

Whether these towns were originally established by the embryo of a new commercial class or by progressive feudal lords to exploit the new needs, they represented a new principle. Unlike the universal relations of dominance and subservience of feudalism, they were free associations of trading people, producing what one representative of the feudal lords called that "new and detestable name", the *commune.*

Within the towns production and trade was organised in guilds, divided on craft lines. These attempted to regulate production, price and quality.

After the Black Death (the terrible plague that spread across Europe in the fourteenth century) had bypassed Poland, the guilds decided to thank the Lord by celebrating more holy days. What they were actually doing, of course, was *sharing out the work* because of the reduction in custom.

The guilds began as bands of equals but, as towns grew in size due to the constant influx of refugee serfs looking for a better life, guild masters were able to make it more difficult for journeymen to join their ranks.

At the same time, merchant guilds were able to exploit their position over the artisan guilds to become an urban elite. Most towns were dominated by a tiny oligarchy, until a series of revolts by poor craftsmen to gain some say in the running of the council took place at the end of the middle ages.

Because of this natural differentiation produced anew by commodity production, the oligarchy in time regained their former status. At the same time all the towns were engaged in battles for a charter of liberties from the landlord class.

As the productivity of labour grew, so did trade, and production for the market, commodity production, and a money economy. Increasingly, grain crops were produced for sale to feed the towns. A stratum of peasants grew rich at their fellows' expense, and aspired to become land-owning farmers producing for a market.

In England, though, it was mainly the feudal lords who took the initiative in reorienting production towards the market. Wool production became more important, and the lords would strive to grab the common lands and expropriate the peasantry.

Serfdom had largely died out in England by the end of the fourteenth century, but bondage to the soil was replaced by short-term leases and an increasing stream of poor peasants being pushed out altogether and forced into vagabondage (roaming the land in search of a living).

By the seventeenth century, it was reckoned that up to quarter of the population was without any means of livelihood other than begging. Progress, as ever, was achieved at the expense of the common people.

Class Struggle Under Feudalism

Whereas the class struggle between patricians and plebians was political, concerned with access to state power, the feudal class stuggle was mainly waged on the economic plane.

A constant, unremitting struggle took place between landlords and peasants. Occasionally this spilt over into revolutionary strife. The Peasants' Revolt of 1381 was the most notable such occasion in England.

After the Black Death, the peasants were in a strong position because of the shortage of labour. The landlords attempted to recoup their losses by enforcing traditional obligations all the harder. This produced a social explosion.

It is significant that the vanguard of the revolutionary peasantry was in the commercial crop areas of the southeast. The development of trade expanded communications and had the effect of binding people together over large areas. Though the revolt was unsuccessful in its immediate objectives, it had the effect of rolling back the predatory ambitions of the feudal lords.

The revolt failed at bottom because the peasantry were a scattered class divided against themselves. King Richard II urged them to "go back to their haymaking", and he hit them on their weak point. It was impossible to maintain the peasantry in a permanent state of mobilisation. Production had developed to a point where only a minority of the population could be maintained as fighting men, while the majority had to work on the land.

This point is illustrated by the Italian peasant revolt, led by Fra Dolcino at a similar time. Though dressed up in religious ideas, the advanced sections of the peasantry developed primitive communist aspirations.

Fra Dolcino and his followers retreated to the Italian Alps. They had to eat and they had to defend themselves. The beginnings of the split in their ranks between fighters and toilers produced demoralisation and defeat.

In this example we can see how the institutions of feudalism corresponded to the then existing state of the productive forces. The miseries of the past have been a necessary travail for mankind.

From Feudalism to Capitalism

Marx called the process of the dissolution of feudalism and emergence of capitalism "primitive accumulation". This process is one of piling up of fortunes in money rather than land on the one hand, and the creation of a propertyless proletariat on the other. It is the separation of the producers from the means by which they can maintain themselves.

We have seen that the feudal peasantry was attached to the land. This guaranteed them a modest subsistence except in times of famine.

Nobody will work for money, with all the insecurity that entails, unless they have to. That is why the imperialists in Africa introduced money poll taxes and, in the case of South Africa drove the Africans on to barren reserves, to force them to provide a supply of wage labour. That is why a monopoly of land in the hands of private owners is a condition for the development of capitalism.

The process by which the peasantry was dispossessed in England was described by Marx in *Capital.* The dissolution of the monasteries, when the church owned one-third of all land, produced an immense mass of ex-monastic paupers. Earlier, the disbandment of the feudal retinues after the Wars of the Roses produced a ferocious breed of vagabonds.

But the main lever of dispossession was the passing of private Acts of Parliament through a parliament of landlords, called Acts of Enclosure. This was simply legalised robbery. It came at a time when the wool trade was expanding, and the landlords wanted more land in order to graze flocks of sheep. Land formerly occupied by perhaps five hundred people was decreed to be the squire's land, and a couple of shepherds took the villagers' place.

Brutal as this process was, it advanced production on the land by doing away with the old inefficient strip system and laying the basis for rational agriculture. Later, the advantages of the industrial revolution, modern machinery, could be applied to these big farms.

The other pole of the process of primitive accumulation was the accumulation of money. The first forms of capital, before industrial capital transformed production, were merchant capital and money-lending capital.

The 'discovery' of America by Spanish plunderers shifted the axis of world trade. Huge fortunes were made in the 'New World'.

The Spanish search for gold was accompanied by the most horrible brutality. Under their rule the numbers of the Indians of San Domingo fell from a population of a million in 1492 to ten thousand in 1530. In Cuba the native population fell from 600,000 in 1492 to only 270 households in 1570.

The merchant capitalist powers outdid one another in their cruelty. Slavery, long thought dead, underwent a renaissance to provide labour for the mines and plantations to serve the world market.

At the same time, the late middle ages saw the rise of great banking families, such as the Fuggers, feeding the needs of the mighty for more and more money. Knights' and princes' feudal revenue could not keep up with the new luxuries available to them. This was clear evidence that production relations on the land were a fetter on the development of the productive forces.

The monarchy too felt the need for more money and began to borrow. So this was the period when every nation began to run up its national debt, which is still with us today and currently standing in Britain at about £100,000 million (1983).

At the end of the middle ages absolutist monarchs like the Tudors in England sprang up in most of the West European countries. These monarchies balanced between the old landed ruling class and the up-and-coming capitalists.

To start with they took society forward by forming strong, stable nation-states within which trade, and hence capitalism, could develop. They defended the interests of merchants abroad in wars of conquest for colonies.

Yet, at bottom, they were out for themselves, and could only flourish because of a deadlock in the class struggle between the capitalists and the landowners. As capitalism developed further, the rising capitalist class conceived ambitions for political power to match their growing economic power. *Bourgeois revolutions* aimed against the reigning absolute monarchs would become necessary for capitalism to consolidate its rule.

Developments parallel to those in agriculture took place in handicraft (manufacturing) production. We have seen how the guilds reflected production relations which originally institutionalised an *advance* in production. Later they became a *barrier,* as capitalists outside the guilds addressed themselves to mobilising wage labour to produce for the ever-increasing markets.

The guilds worked on the principle of limiting production to keep up prices, and used their traditional privileges to resist inroads. Merchant capitalists moved in to lap up the surplus labour of peasant households half-employed on tiny plots of land. They began to 'put out' weaving to these households.

The peasantry became more and more dependent on their weaving income. The merchants were able to move from just supplying raw materials and supplying sales outlets, to possession of the peasants, looms and even their cottages. Through their control over outlets they held the whip hand.

This was another important process whereby the feudal peasantry was reduced to proletarian status.

Throughout the sixteenth and seventeenth centuries, handicraft workshops were set up. It was found that the job could be broken down into simple processes. Adam Smith begins his *Wealth of Nations* by explaining the division of labour in making pins, through which an enormous amount of pins could be cheaply produced compared with the old skilled processes.

More than that, the breaking down of the job into simple repetitive tasks provided the possibility of replacing manual labour with machines. Starting by taking production as it found it, capitalism was beginning to revolutionise the instruments of production.

Capitalism could not move straight into domination of the world economy without hindrance. The newly awakened productive forces were in revolt at the old relations of production. These had to be overcome and new production relations installed which corresponded to the stage of development of the productive forces.

This was the task of the bourgeois revolutions. The English Revolution of the 1640s, the American Revolution of 1776, and the French Revolution of 1789-94 were the decisive struggles which laid the foundations for the domination of capitalism on a world scale.

What precisely were the tasks of these bourgeois revolutions?

Though feudalism was no longer dominant, the landed interest remained a fetter on commodity production.

Though in England the land-owning gentry switched to production for the market, in France up till 1789 the aristocracy guzzled a large part of the surplus in rents, and used their privileged position to impose all kinds of tolls on the free movement of goods.

This raised prices for everyone and enabled the bourgeoisie, in opposing the aristocracy, to claim to represent the interests of the nation as a whole. Up till the storming of the Bastille by the Parisian masses in 1789, for instance, food entering Paris was subject to a toll as a feudal privilege.

France was the classic country of the bourgeois revolution, where the old aristocracy was completely swept aside. The peasantry, increasingly producing for a market, had a tendency after the bourgeois revolution of 1789 to become divided into an aspiring capitalist class and a propertyless class of rural wage labourers.

Capitalism also had the task of setting up centralised national economies as an envelope within which the new mode of production could develop.

Germany as late as the nineteenth century showed the necessity for capitalist production to have a stable nation-state. Germany was still divided into thirty-six statelets on the eve of the 1848 revolution, each originally having its own currency, its own system of tolls and tariffs, its own weights, land measures and local communications.

Clearly this confusion of small states provided an almost impenetrable barrier to the development of large scale, all-German industry and trade. The failure of the German bourgeoisie to carry through "their own" revolution, because of their fear of the new working class behind them, led to these tasks being carried out under the hegemony of the Prussian *junkers* (landlords) around Bismarck—who saw the need to build a modern capitalist nation.

In Britain and France, on the other hand, national unification had already been substantially carried out by the absolutist monarchies as one of the progressive tasks of developing the framework of capitalist development.

Nor was the old aristocracy the only section to resist progress. A section of the capitalists, who had originally taken society forward, became increasingly reactionary. Rich merchants used their influence on the kings to gain monopolies in trade. They used their privileges to raise the price of commodities.

These reactionary capitalists were opposed by the smaller merchants, who were forced to fight for free trade, and by the urban masses. Likewise, big moneylenders made their money by lending to the crown, and thus were dependent on the monarchy.

The capitalist class as a whole was now strong enough to bid for political power, which it needed to complete its revolution. The absolutist monarchies, from being a shield to defend the expansion of trade, had become an obstacle. They had to be done away with; and the masses of artisans and yeomen were mobilisded to do the job for the capitalist class.

Capitalism

Capitalists measure their wealth not in land or slaves, but in money. The money fortunes found their way into production in the industrial revolution, a period as significant for mankind as the agricultural revolution thousands of years earlier.

Capitalism is a system of *exploitation* like feudalism or slavery. Its distinctive feature is that rather than just consuming the surplus, the capitalists are forced by the nature of their system to plough the bulk of it back into production.

Capitalism thus achieves a dynamic unheard of in earlier epochs. Instead of just exploiting more people, as feudal lords strove to do through never-ending wars, capitalism exploits people more—it *develops the productivity of labour.*

In so doing it provides the *possibility* of a society of abundance, and doing away altogether with the division between exploiter and exploited. It provides, in other words, the possibility of a *higher stage* of society than capitalism itself.

Capitalism bases itself on the monopoly of the means of production in the hands of the ruling capitalist class. The vast majority of people are cut off from the means of life unless they work on terms dictated by the capitalist class.

Formally, wage workers seem to be paid for the work they do. In reality they are exploited as much as the feudal serf or the slave.

Under capitalism, labour-power (the capacity of the worker to labour) is a commodity like any other, in that it is bought and sold on the market. It is sold by its owner, the worker, and bought by the owner of money, the capitalist.

But labour-power is different from other commodities in this respect: it has the unique property of being able to *create value.* This is its usefulness to the capitalist, this is why the capitalist buys labour-power (employs workers).

As labour-power is consumed in production (as workers are put to work) value is created far in excess of what the capitalist has paid (as wages) for the labour-power. This is the source of the capitalist's profit.

If labour-power is to be available in the market place, so that the capitalist can buy it, labour-power must be *produced.* "Given the individual," Marx wrote, "the production of labour-power consists in his reproduction of himself, or his maintenance". Marx adds immediately that this maintenance contains "a historical and moral element"—i.e., what a working-class family require for their maintenance, and for the raising of children as a new generation of wage-workers, will depend on standards of living which have been established through struggle as acceptable to the working class in that society.

The essence of capitalist exploitation is this: *The worker is paid wages not for his/her labour but for his/her labour-power—his/her keep.* The difference is taken by the capitalist.

Thus the worker's daily work is divided into "necessary labour" and "surplus labour". The worker performs "necessary labour" during that part of the day spent in producing value which, when sold, will cover the cost of the wages. The worker performs "surplus labour" during the remainder of the working day, producing value which, when sold, will cover the rent, interest and profit which goes to the capitalist class.

Capitalism at first strove to increase the rate of exploitation through enforcing repeated increases in the working day (the workers were usually paid by the day, however many hours they worked). The capitalists were able to get away with this because of the almost endless *reserve army of labour* created by the destruction of petty production in town and country, and the driving of hordes of starving poor into the cities.

This meant that workers had to work on almost any terms dictated by the bosses. But the capitalist system was in danger of killing the goose that laid the golden egg. Surveys undertaken in Britain during the 1850s showed a stunted, prematurely enfeebled race of workers unfit for military service.

In the nineteenth century, British workers began the struggle for the legal limitation of the working day, what Marx called "the first victory for the political economy of the working class". We must note, though, that, like later reforms such as the National Health Service—the Ten Hours Act was also in the long-term interests of the ruling class because it maintained a labour supply in fit condition.

Nevertheless, because of the short-sighted greed of capitalists, these reforms were only enforced through struggle in the teeth of ruling-class opposition.

Thus, thwarted from indefinitely increasing the rate of surplus-value through what Marx called the extraction of *absolute surplus value* (e.g., by increasing the working day), the capitalists were forced to move to increasing the rate of exploitation through the extraction of *relative surplus-value.*

This means, instead of getting more hours of labour out of the workers, they had to raise the productivity of the workers' labour—to get more output from the same hours of work.

The more productive labour is, the less of the working day needs to be devoted to producing the value of the necessities of life for the workers (their wages), and the more time can be devoted to producing surplus for the capitalist.

The motor of capitalism is competition. Each capitalist has to undercut his competitors if he is to survive. The best way to sell cheaper is to produce cheaper. Since labour-time is the measure of value, that means producing with less labour-time.

Mechanising is the main means of continually raising the productivity of labour. Perhaps the best example of the process is the one supplied by Marx—the case of the hand-loom weavers.

The invention of the spinning jenny, and the mass-production of cheaper yarn, led to the mechanisation of cloth-making. Weaving, up to then, had still been a handicraft process. As demand for weavers expanded in the early years of the industrial revolution, the hand-loom weavers were able to bid up their wages and become a regular 'aristocracy of labour'. For capitalism they represented an obstacle to cheap production. Inevitably, as a result, the power loom was invented, for capitalist necessity is the mother and father of invention.

It would be quite clear to any casual observer that the power loom took much less labour-time to produce an equivalent amount of woven cloth.

In vain did the hand-loom weavers bid the price of their product down. In no way could they compete with the power loom.

At their peak there had been a quarter of a million hand-loom weavers. Over a generation they were wiped out with thousands actually dying of starvation. A much smaller number were able to get jobs, at lower rates of pay, supervising the power looms.

That has ever been the way with capitalist progress. But in this way capitalism has developed the fantastic productive powers of modern industry.

Capitalism also develops a form of the state appropriate to its own rule. Different forms of state can exist under capitalism, each corresponding to a different stage in the development of the class struggle—from parliamentary democracy to fascism and bonapartist military-police dictatorships of the most variegated kinds.

All these forms of state have **one thing** in common—in the last analysis they defend private property in the means of production, and therefore the rule of capital.

Marx and Engels often emphasised that democracy is the ideal form of capitalist class rule, first because it enables the capitalists to sort out their differences; and secondly because it gives the working-class parties a semblance of a say of running society. Changes necessary for the continued existence of the system can thus more easily be made.

At the same time bourgeois democracy provides the most favourable ground for the workers to organise to overthrow their exploiters.

Capitalism has required, as a precondition of its existence, a new class of propertyless toilers. Throughout its development capitalism has created a bigger and bigger pool of wage-workers.

Even since the Second World War, millions of small farmers have been driven from the land in countries such as France, Italy and Japan. This has been a progressive step in so far as it tears these people away from the isolation and backwardness of rural life, and in so far as it represents a raising of the productivity of labour, so that less people are needed to grow food and more can set their hands to producing other things.

But, at the same time, capitalism has no regard for the interests of people, and relentlessly searches out surplus value at any cost to the masses.

The Capitalist World Market

As we have seen, though it has created misery for the masses, capitalism has been a dynamic system. Its aim and impulse is more and more surplus value.

Thus industrial capitalism strives to conquer the world. Merchant capital had contented itself with exacting tribute from the existing modes of production in other countries; industrial capital, in the empires it created after the industrial revolution, flooded these countries with cheap manufactured goods.

These goods necessarily destroyed the existing system of handicrafts, which was united with agriculture in the villages. Existing societies were forcibly broken up. Moreover agriculture was increasingly switched towards the requirements of the world market. Capitalism was beginning to create a world after its own image.

This process was brought to its highest stage in the imperialist phase of capitalist development.

The different phases through which capitalist countries entered into relations with pre-capitalist nations—and in exploiting them, drew them into the orbit of capitalism, can be seen clearly in the case of India.

In the first instance India was colonised not by the British government but by the East India Company, an association of merchants. They made fortunes for themselves by monopolising Anglo-Indian trade, buying cheap and selling dear. They also strove to grab the internal trade of India, and under their greedy control the price of grain sky-rocketed during famines—beyond the reach of the needy.

The period of domination of the East India Company corresponded to the requirements of primitive accumulation in Britain. Money fortunes were made by the merchant adventurers through unequal exchange. After the Battle of Plassey, which gave Britain sway over the entire Indian subcontinent, the Bank of England printed £10 and £15 notes for the first time. The conservative historian, Burke, estimated that plunder from India between 1757 and 1780 amounted to £40 million, a huge figure for that time.

British capitalism was not always an advocate of international free trade. That came later, when Britain had a monopoly of large-scale capitalist production. In fact, Indian textiles imported into Britain had duties of 70% to 80% imposed on them right up to about 1830.

It was only when the Lancashire machine textile industry had built up an unassailable position that restrictions were lifted because they were no longer necessary. The Indian market was then flooded with cheap cotton goods, and its own textile producers ruined.

The fate of Indian society was now bound up with the development of competitive capitalism. Incidentally, British capitalism did not hesitate to resort to the most barbarous methods of imposing their exports upon the Indians. For instance, the hands of weavers in Dacca were cut off! Terrible famine stalked the area, and the whole region became partly overgrown with jungle.

In 1850 India absorbed one quarter of Lancashire textiles. After the Indian Mutiny, which began in 1857, the British rulers saw the need to build up a network of railways, to allow rapid troop movements, in order to keep the population pinned down. This marked the beginning of the third phase of the exploitation of India. Export of capital rather than of goods became the predominant feature.

Imperialism

This development was the result of the growth of monopoly capitalism in the metropolitan countries, involving the fusion of finance with manufacturing capital—the epoch of *imperialism,* which was analysed by Lenin. National markets became too small for the giant monopolies as they swallowed up their weaker competitors, expanded production to new heights, and looked for new and profitable areas for investment.

In the case of India, this process really got going at the end of the nineteenth century when capital was exported from Britain to build up a modern Indian-based textile industry, mainly under British ownership.

"One capitalist kills many", as Marx says. Capitalism destroys not only petty production, but also continually bankrupts the weakest of its own brethren and jettisons them into the ranks of the propertyless.

This is a two-sided process—progressive in its objective economic content, by piling up enormous productive resources for the potential benefit of mankind, but, under capitalism, concentrating collosal power in the hands of a tiny handful of rich magnates.

At the end of the nineteenth century we saw the development of monopoly out of competition itself.

The banking system, Marx wrote, "places all the available and even potential capital of society that is not already actively employed at the disposal of the industrial and commercial capitalists, so that neither the lenders nor users of this capital are its real owners or producers. It thus does away with the private character of capital and thus contains in itself, but only in itself, the abolition of capital itself... Finally there is no doubt that the credit system will serve as a powerful lever during the transition from the capitalist mode of production to the mode of production of associated labour, but only as one element in connection with other great organic revolutions of the mode of production itself."

Capitalism continually requires infusions of money capital in order for profit-making to continue uninterruptedly. Once a stock of commodities has been produced, a single capitalist would either have to wait till he had sold them before he once again had money in his pocket to restart production; or he would have to keep stocks of money-capital idle much of the time as a reserve for investment when needed; he would have to continually pay money into a fund to renew stocks of fixed capital *which might be idle for ten or twenty years.*

In reality, a stratum of capitalist hangers-on develop, not prepared to invest directly in production, but quite prepared to lend their money in order to cut themselves a slice of the pie of surplus-value. So there is a tendency for competition to generate unused reserves of money capital. These reserves are collected in a few rich hands—concentrations of *finance capital.*

Finance capital initially provided a stimulus to the capitalist system by gathering and syphoning money-capital into production. It did so, of course, only to cream off an increasing proportion of the surplus value for itself.

As Marx pointed out, finance capital also concentrates tremendous economic power in its own hands, and effectively integrates the individual manufacturing capitalist into the requirements of capitalist production as a whole through allocation and withdrawal of credits.

Imperialism is the epoch in which finance capital has fused with monopoly capital involved in production.

Under imperialism, while competition between capitalists within the boundaries of the nation-state has not been completely done away with, conflict has spilt over into the international arena.

The big monopolies and the banks exported capital rather than just commodities. A massive programme of railway building was undertaken in every continent and clime. Loans were floated for the most far-flung places. A systematic search was undertaken for every kind of raw material and mineral resource.

Conflicts now began between national capital blocs. The struggle was for nothing less than mastery of the world. Wars unparalleled in ferocity in the history of mankind broke out for colonies and a redivision of imperial spoils.

The First World War indicated that capitalism, like previous forms of class society, had ceased to be progressive. Instead of taking production forward, there was mass destruction and mass murder.

But at the same time, a new society was developing within the old. The Russian revolution served notice that the rule of the working class was at hand.

Revolutionary Role of the Working Class

The working class is unlike any other exploited class in history. We have seen how the three-sided class struggle within slave society necessarily led to the "common ruin of the contending classes". We have seen how the feudal peasantry were for hundreds of years incapable of formulating a coherent revolutionary alternative to the system that exploited them.

This failure had not been accidental. The peasantry is an isolated class, scattered over the countryside and finds itself very difficult to combine. But their problem is not just geographical, it is at bottom social. For as Marx put it, the peasantry is a class only in one sense:

"in so far as millions of families live under economic conditions of existence that separate their mode of life, their interests and their culture from those of the other classes, and put them in hostile opposition to the latter, they form a class. In so far as... the identity of their interests begets no community, no national bond and no political organisation among them, they do not form a class."

For the peasantry are smallholders—a class divided against itself. They are like potatoes in a sack—destined for the chipping machine under capitalist progress.

The working class, on the other hand, is concentrated in great masses by the very nature of factory production. Unlike the peasantry, their only strength lies in collective action. Through collective exploitation, the working class are trained and educated by capitalism itself to act as the system's grave-diggers.

Nor is the modern working class left to vegetate at a modest but constant standard of living. Insecurity is a condition of their existence.

Capitalism has produced many wonders inconceivable hitherto. It has also produced social disasters inconceivable under previous forms of society—crises taking the form of *overproduction*.

In pre-capitalist societies, the subsistence of the toilers was only interrupted by famine—physical shortage of necessities. Primitive people's minds may well have been clogged with all sorts of superstition, but the spectacle of people starving, while sitting idly in front of the tools necessary to make the things they need, is a unique product of our society.

Capitalism is *social* production. It is social in two ways. Firstly, it ties the whole world up into one economic unit through the world market, a worldwide division of labour. Everybody is dependent on everyone else for the things they need.

Secondly it introduces large scale production only workable by collective labour.

Yet, at the same time, the system runs on *private* appropriation *and private profit.* It is anarchic—nobody knows how much of any commodity is needed at any time. The capitalist plans production within his own factory, but social production as a whole is *unplanned.*

Marx wrote: "Capitalist production seeks continually to overcome these immanent barriers but overcomes them only by means which again place the barriers in its way and on a more formidable scale. The real barrier of capitalist production is capital itself". *(Capital* Vol.3)

"The same bourgeois mind which praises division of labour in the workshop, life-long annexation of the labourer to a partial operation and his complete subjection to capital, as being an organisation of labour that increases its productiveness—that same bourgeois mind denounces with equal vigour every conscious attempt to socially control and regulate the process of production, as an inroad upon such sacred things as the rights of property, freedom and unrestricted play for the bent of the individual capitalist. It is very characteristic that the enthusiastic apologists of the factory system have nothing more damning to urge against a general organisation of the labour of society than that it would turn all society into one immense factory". *(Capital* Vol.I)

How is 'overproduction' possible? The reason people can't just walk into the factories, and start producing the things they want, is because they don't own those factories: and the state defends the property interests of the ruling class.

The ruling class, for their part, produce only to make profit. No profit, no jobs.

Every worker laid off by one capitalist means one less consumer for another capitalist's goods. So crisis, triggered off in any one major sector of the economy, can radiate throughout the system.

Crises of mass unemployment are as much a creation of capitalism as Coca Cola.

The laws of capitalism work, "despite anarchy, in and through anarchy". Each capitalist is oblivious to the actual requirements of society for pig-iron or knicker-elastic at any time. They produce what they hope will make the maximum profit, whether pig-iron or knicker-elastic. They organise production within their factory; but anarchy reigns in production as a whole.

The possibility of crisis is inherent in such a system. All that socialists want to do is plan production in society at large in the same meticulous way the capitalists do within each separate factory.

The worker, unlike the exploited classes in pre-capitalist society, is a free person—free in that he is not subject to "relations of personal dependence" and can work for any boss he likes, and free from any attachment to the means of subsistence. But the workers' expectations and feelings of security are continually shattered by plagues of mass unemployment.

Crisis poses over and over again before the working class the need to change society. Capitalism will never collapse of its own accord. It has to be overthrown.

It is a caricature of Marxism to suggest that the revolution will be made automatically by workers made destitute by the workings of the system. It will be overthrown by a *conscious and determined class,* not just by a desperate class.

What is true is that the perpetual insecurity of existence under capitalism will produce a questioning in the minds of workers. Just as we have to understand nature in order to master it, so workers will have to understand the nature of their enemy before they can overthrow it.

That is why we are producing this pamphlet.

We have outlined the progress of mankind from primitive communism to capitalism. An objective look at the record shows also the world we have lost. Chief Sitting Bull, an outstanding defender of Native American tribal society, ended up miserably as a kind of freak in Buffalo Bill's Wild West Show. As he toured the Western capitals he was astounded at the wealth—but also at the poverty. He said, "The white man (by which he meant the capitalist system) knows how to produce wealth, not how to distribute it".

Yet the possibility now exists for a society where enough can be produced for each to take according to their need. The possibilities posed before mankind by science and new technology were foreseen by Marx over 120 years ago. In one of his notebooks he wrote:

"No longer does the worker insert a modified natural thing as middle link between the object and himself; rather he inserts the process of nature, transformed into an industrial process, as a means between himself and unorganic nature mastering it. In this transformation it is...the development of the social individual which appears as the great foundation-stone of production and of wealth. The theft of alien labour-time, on which the present is based, appears a miserable foundation in face of this new one, created by large-scale industry itself...

"The surplus labour of the mass has ceased to be the condition for the development of general wealth, just as the non-labour of the few, for the development of the human head... The free development of individuals and hence...the general reduction of the necessary labour of society to a minimum, which then corresponds to the artistic, scientific, etc., development of the individuals in the time set free, and with the means created, for all of them." *(Grundrisse)*.

The !Kung people in the Kalahari live lives of material want and intellectual backwardness by our standards, but they know better than to make labour for others the driving force of their society. In consequence they work a week of between 12 and 19 hours!

Now mankind has the resources and technical means to reach a society of abundance. The working class, organised and conscious, can overthrow capitalism and create such a society—a society where people can plan what they need and want, produce it, and then spend the rest of the time enjoying it. It's as simple as that.

ENGELS LETTER TO J. BLOCH, LONDON, SEPTEMBER 21, 1890

According to the materialist conception of history, the *ultimately* determining element in history is the production and reproduction of real life. Other than this neither Marx nor I have ever asserted. Hence if somebody twists this into saying that the economic element is the *only* determining one, he transforms that proposition into a meaningless, abstract, senseless phrase. The economic situation is the basis, but the various elements of the superstructure—political forms of the class struggle and its results, to wit: constitutions established by the victorious class after a successful battle, etc., juridical forms, and even the reflexes of all these actual struggles in the brains of the participants, political, juristic, philosophical theories, religious views and their further development into systems of dogmas—also exercise their influence upon the course of the historical struggles and in many cases preponderate in determining their *form*. There is an interaction of all these elements in which, amid all the endless host of accidents (that is, of things and events whose inner interconnection is so remote or so impossible of proof that we can regard it as non-existent, as negligible), the economic movement finally asserts itself as necessary. Otherwise the application of the theory to any period of history would be easier than the solution of a simple equation of the first degree.

We make our history ourselves, but, in the first place, under very definite assumptions and conditions. Among these the economic ones are ultimately decisive. But the political ones, etc., and indeed even the traditions which haunt human minds also play a part, although not the decisive one. The Prussian state also arose and developed from historical, ultimately economic, causes. But it could scarcely be maintained without pedantry that among the many small states of North Germany, Brandenburg was specifically determined by economic necessity to become the great power embodying the economic, linguistic and, after the Reformation, also the religious difference between North and South, and not by other elements as well (above all by its entanglement with Poland, owing to the possession of Prussia, and hence with international political relations—which were indeed also decisive in the formation of the Austrian dynastic power). Without making oneself ridiculous it would be a difficult thing to explain in terms of economics the existence of every small state in Germany, past and present, or the origin of the High German consonant permutations, which widened the geographic partition wall formed by the mountains from the Sudetic range to the Taunus to form a regular fissure across all Germany.

In the second place, however, history is made in such a way that the final result always arises from conflicts between many individual wills, of which each in turn has been made what it is by a host of particular conditions of life. Thus there are innumerable intersecting force, an infinite series of parallelograms of forces which give rise to one resultant—the historical event. This may again itself be viewed as the product of a power which works as a whole *unconsciously* and without volition. For what each individual wills is obstructed by everyone else, and what emerges is something that no one willed. Thus history has proceeded hitherto in the manner of a natural process and is essentially subject to the same laws of motion. But from the fact that the wills of individuals — each of whom desires what he is impelled to by his physical constitution and external, in the last resort economic, circumstances (either his own personal circumstances or those of society in general)—do not attain what they want, but are merged into an aggregate mean, a common resultant, it must not be concluded that they are equal to zero. On the contrary, each contributes to the resultant and is to this extent included in it.

I would furthermore ask you to study this theory from its original sources and not at second-hand; it is really much easier. Marx hardly wrote anything in which it did not play a part. But especially *The Eighteenth Brumaire of Louis Bonaparte* is a most excellent example of its application. There are also many allusion to it in *Capital*. Then may I also direct you to my writings: *Herr Eugen Duhring's Revolution in Science* and *Ludwig Feuerbach and the end of Classical German Philosophy* in which I have given the most detailed account of historical material which, as far as I know, exists. [*The German Ideology* was not published in Marx or Engels lifetime]

Marx and I are ourselves partly to blame for the fact that the younger people sometimes lay more stress on the economic side than is due to it. We had to emphasise the main principle *vis-á-vis* our adversaries, who denied it, and we had not always the time, the place or the opportunity to give their due to the other elements involved in the interaction. But when it came to presenting a section of history, that is, to making a practical application, it was a different matter and there no error was permissible. Unfortunately, however, it happens only too often that people think they have fully understood a new theory and can apply it without more ado from the moment they have assimilated its main principles, and even those not always correctly. And I cannot exempt many of the more recent

"Marxists" from this reproach, for the most amazing rubbish has been produced in this quarter, too....

FROM LUDWIG FEUERBACH AND THE END OF CLASSICAL GERMAN PHILOSOPHY BY ENGELS (EXTRACT)

Men make their own history, whatever its outcome may be, in that each person follows his own consciously desired end, and it is precisely the resultant of these many wills operating in different directions, and of their manifold effects upon the outer world, that constitutes history. Thus it is also a question of what the many individuals desire. The will is determined by passion or deliberation. But the levers which immediately determine passion or deliberation are of very different kinds. Partly they may be external objects, partly ideal motives, ambition, "enthusiasm for truth and justice", personal hatred, or even purely individual whims of all kinds. But, on the one hand, we have seen that the many individual wills active in history for the most part produce results quite other than those intended—often quite the opposite; that their motives, therefore, in relation to the total result are likewise of only secondary importance. On the other hand, the further question arises: What driving forces in turn stand behind these motives? What are the historical forces which transform themselves into these motives in the brains of the actors?

The old materialism never put this question to itself. Its conception of history, in so far as it has one at all, is therefore essentially pragmatic; it divides men who act in history into noble and ignoble and then finds that as a rule the noble are defrauded and the ignoble are victorious. hence, it follows for the old materialism that nothing very edifying is to be got from the study of history, and for us that in the realm of history the old materialism becomes untrue to itself because it takes the ideal driving forces which operate there as ultimate causes, instead of investigating what is behind them, what are the driving forces of these driving forces. This inconsistency does not lie in the fact that *ideal* driving forces are recognized, but in the investigation not being carried further back behind these into their motive causes. On the other hand, the philosophy of history, particularly as represented by Hegel, recognizes that the ostensible and also the really operating motives of men who act in history are by no means the ultimate causes of historical events; that behind these motives are other motive powers, which have to be discovered. But it does not seek these powers in history itself, it imports them rather from outside, from philosophical ideology, into history. Hegel, for example, instead of explaining the history of ancient Greece out of its own inner interconnections, simply maintains that it is nothing more than the working out of "forms of beautiful individuality", the realization of a "work of art" as such. He says much in this connection about the old Greeks that is fine and profound, but that does not prevent us today from refusing to be put off with such an explanation, which is a mere manner of speech.

When, therefore, it is a question of investigating the driving powers which—consciously or unconsciously, and indeed very often unconsciously—lie behind the motives of men who act in history and which constitute the real ultimate driving forces of history, then it is not a question so much of the motives of single individuals, however eminent, as of those motives which set in motion great masses, whole people, and again whole classes of the people in each people; and this, too, not merely for an instant, like the transient flaring up of a straw-fire which quickly dies down, but as a lasting action resulting in a great historical transformation. To ascertain the driving causes which here in the minds of acting masses and their leaders—to so-called great men—are reflected as conscious motives, clearly or unclearly, directly or in an ideological, even glorified, form—is the only path which can put us on the track of the laws holding sway both in history as a whole, and at particular periods and in particular lands. Everything which sets men in motion must go through their minds; but what form it will take in the mind will depend very much upon the circumstances. The workers have by no means become reconciled to capitalist machine industry, even though they no longer simply break the machines to pieces, as they still did in 1848 on the Rhine.

PREFACE OF A CONTRIBUTION TO THE CRITIQUE OF POLITICAL ECONOMY BY MARX (EXTRACT)

In the social production of their life, men enter into definite relations that are indispensable and independent of their will, relations of production which correspond to a definite stage of development of their material productive forces. The sum total of these relations of production constitutes the economic structure of society, the real foundation, on which rises a legal and political superstructure and to which correspond definite forms of social consciousness.

The mode of production of material life conditions the social, political and intellectual life process in general. It is not the consciousness of men that determines their being, but, on the contrary, their social being that determines their consciousness.

At a certain stage of their development, the material productive forces of society come in conflict with the existing relations of production, or—what is but a legal expression for the same thing—with the property relations within which they have been at work hitherto. From forms of development of the productive forces these relations turn into their fetters.

Then begins an epoch of social revolution. With the change of the economic foundation the entire immense superstructure is more or less rapidly transformed. In considering such transformations a distinction should always be made between the material transformation of the economic conditions of production, which can be determined with the precision of natural science, and the legal, political, religious, aesthetic or philosophic—in short, ideological forms in which men become conscious of this conflict and fight it out. Just as our opinion of an individual is not based on what he thinks of himself, so can we not judge of such a period of transformation by its own consciousness; on the contrary, this consciousness must be explained rather from the contradictions of material life, from the existing conflict between the social productive forces and the relations of production.

No social order ever perishes before all the productive forces for which there is room in it have developed; and new, higher relations of production never appear before the material conditions of their existence have matured in the womb of the old society itself. Therefore mankind always sets itself only such tasks as it can solve; since, looking at the matter more closely, it will always be found that the tasks itself arises only when the material conditions of its solution already exist or are at least in the process of formation.

In broad outlines Asiatic, ancient, feudal, and modern bourgeois modes of production can be designated as progressive epochs in the economic formation of society. The bourgeois relations of production are the last antagonistic form of the social process of production—antagonistic not in the sense of individual antagonisms, but of one arising from the social conditions of life of the individuals; at the same time the productive forces developing in the womb of bourgeois society create the material conditions for the solution of that antagonism. This social formation brings, therefore, the prehistory of society to a close.

Questions on Historical Materialism

1) What separates human beings from other animals?
2) What determines our consciousness, our ideas, and our view of the world?
3) What role do Marxists explain is played by individuals in history?
4) What do we mean by 'class'?
5) How long did human beings exist before society was divided into classes, and what caused that division?
6) Which group of people constituted the first ruling class and why?
7) What was the Asiatic Mode of Production?
8) What were the causes of the decline and fall of Roman slave society?
9) In what way did the exploitation of serfs differ from that of slaves?
10) What ultimately undermined the class struggle of the peasantry against the landlords during feudal times?
11) What did Marx mean by "primative accumulation"?
12) What part did the "revolutionising of the means of production" play in the development of capitalism?
13) Describe some modern-day examples of this process.
14) What were the tasks of the bourgeois revolutions?
15) What differentiates capitalism from earlier systems of exploitation?
16) How does the exploitation of the wage worker differ from that of the serf?
17) Explain what Marxists mean by "Imperialism".
18) During what period did capitalism cease to play a progressive role?
19) Why did Marx described the working class as the "gravediggers" of capitalism?
20) What are the tasks of the proletarian, socialist revolution?

Suggested reading

The Communist Manifesto, Marx and Engels
The German Ideology, Marx and Engels
The Origin of the Family, Private Property and the State, Engels
Socialism: Utopian and Scientific, Engels
The Part Played by Labour in the Transition from Ape to Man, Engels
The Three Sources and Three Component Parts of Marxism, Lenin
The History of the Russian Revolution (3 volumes), Trotsky
The Civil War in France, Marx
The Peasant War in Germany, Engels (online)

The Eighteenth Brumaire of Louis Bonaparte, Marx
The Holy Family, Marx (online)
Ludwig Feuerbach and the End of Classical German Philosophy, Engels,
The Poverty of Philosophy, Marx
The Development of the Monist View of History, Plekhanov (online)
The Foundations of Christianity, Kautsky
On Marx and Engels, Lenin
Preface and Introduction to a contribution to the critique of Political Economy, Marx
The Critique of the Gotha Programme, Marx
Historical articles at Marxist.com

Obtainable from Wellred Books, PO Box 50525, London E14 6WG
Or at the online Marxist bookshop at wellred.marxist.com
An important Marxist online resouce is at marxists.org

Marxist Economics

By Mick Brooks

"Every child knows a nation which ceased to work, I will not say for a year, but even for a few weeks, would perish. Every child knows, too, that the masses of products corresponding to the different needs required different and quantitatively determined masses of the total labour of society. That this *necessity* of the *distribution* of social labour in definite proportions cannot possibly be done away with by a *particular form* of social production but can only change the *mode* of its *appearance*, is self-evident. No natural laws can be done away with. What can change in historically different circumstances is only the *form* in which these laws assert themselves. And the form in which this proportional distribution of labour asserts itself, in the state of society where the interconnection of social labour is manifested in the *private exchange* of the individual products of labour, is precisely the *exchange value* of these products." (Marx to Kugelmann, July 11, 1868, shortly after the publication of *Capital*.)

When looking at historical materialism, the Marxist theory of historical development as a whole, we ask the question: what differentiates humans from other animals? We find that humans differentiate themselves by transforming themselves and external nature. The process by which people define and redefine themselves is the labour process. Sure, humans are thinking beings. But why do they need to develop the capacity for thought? What are they thinking about? Usually they are thinking about survival, about where the next meal is coming from. Marxists argue that the way people organise themselves to gain their daily bread is the mode of production, the skeleton of any form of society. And insofar as we can talk of an objective notion of progress in human history, it is given by the development of the productive forces, which in turn is achieved by raising the productivity of labour, the increase of our power over external nature.

The "Magic" of the Marketplace

Now to the capitalist mode of production. Capitalism is mystifying to understand. The cause of our mystification is the market system. Capitalism presents itself to us as a system of universal commodity production (that is, where everything is produced for sale) where even labour power is a commodity. That is how Marx defined capitalism. We hear a lot about the "magic of the marketplace". Once in place, a system where everything is bought and sold strikes us as eternal and natural. We need to remind ourselves that generalised commodity production is a late and recent development in social evolution. For hundreds of thousands of years humans made their living without the aid of markets.

Secondly we need to understand what markets do. They are a form of the social division of labour, as explained by Marx. But that is not how they appear to us. A worker in Malaysia gets a job on a dredger, which is digging out tin ore from the river. After passing through dozens of sets of hands the tin ends up in Taiwan, where it is used to make solder to manufacture a transistor radio. Meanwhile a garment worker in Milan machines a piece of cloth that began life as raw cotton in the field of a peasant in Pakistan. The peasant is very poor. All he has to listen to at night is the transistor radio. He doesn't know about the workers in Malaysia or the woman in the sweatshop in Taiwan with the electric soldering iron. He doesn't know about the catwalks in Milan and the illegal immigrant on the outskirts who turned the raw cotton he grew with his own hands into a luxury item.

What is going on here is a division of labour, indeed a global division of labour. But nobody sits down in a meeting and says: "Here's what we need. Here's how long it takes to get it. You're good at this, why don't you do this? You're good at that, why don't you do that? OK, let's vote on it. We've got agreement; let's do it." The worker in Malaysia would like to be a teacher, but it's not to be. He has a family to feed. The woman in Taiwan would probably prefer not to spend long hours looking at circuit boards doing her eyesight in. The market is a ferocious dictator, but no one person takes decisions. It just happens, or so it seems. None of these economic actors (as economists call people) realise how everyone is dependent on everyone else. The forces of supply and demand, we are told, act as signals. Nobody knows how much tin we all need at the moment. But if too little is being produced, the price will go up because of shortages. If the price goes up there is a super-profit to be made. And where there is a super-profit, there will be an inflow of capital. Capitalists making average or below average profits in other sectors of the economy will be attracted to tin production. To keep pumping the stuff out of the factory gate they will be prepared to hire more workers. They may even have to post higher wages, to attract workers from other industries. The system is unplanned. But the capital will keep on flowing in as long as there is money to be made. This is what Adam Smith called the "invisible hand" in celebrating market forces. As more capital flows in the price of tin will be beaten down and the rate of profit in that sector return to the average. Quite often capitalists will overshoot, respond to the shortage by overproducing, leading to unsold stocks and bankruptcies. Capitalism, which is held up to us as the apex of efficiency, necessarily and always wastes human and material resources through its planlessness. The boss wouldn't let you get away with this in "his" factory! But the system, we are told, works itself!

Two divisions of labour

The market is not the only division of labour. In 1937 Ronald Coase, a right-wing economist, posed the question that if markets are so wonderful "why a firm emerges at all in a specialised exchange economy?" He goes on. "It is convenient if in searching for a definition of a firm, we first consider the economic system as it is naturally treated by the economist... The normal economic system works itself. For its current operation it is under no central control, it needs no central survey. Over the whole range of human activity and human need, supply is adjusted to demand, and production to consumption, by a process that is automatic, elastic and responsive. An economist thinks of the economic system as being co-ordinated by the price mechanism, and society becomes not an organisation but an organism." (We shall see later what an idealised view this is of the workings of capitalism, but for the moment bear with it.) After setting forward the conventional view of the magic of the marketplace, Coase goes on. "Within a firm the description does not fit at all... If a workman moves from department Y to department X, he does not go because of a change in relative prices, but because he is ordered to do so."

Way before Coase, Marx had realised that there are two divisions of labour within a capitalist economy, one in the marketplace and the other within the firm. "The very same bourgeois mentality which extols the manufacturing division of labour, the life-long annexation of the worker to a partial operation, and the unconditional subordination of the detail worker to capital, extols them as an organisation of labour which increases productivity - denounces just as loudly every kind of deliberate social control and regulation of the social process of production, denounces it as an invasion of the inviolable property rights, liberty and self-determining genius of the individual capitalist. It is characteristic that the inspired apologists of the factory system can find nothing worse to say of any proposal for the general organisation of social labour, than that it would transform the whole of society into a factory." (*Capital*)

Both divisions of labour just impose themselves on us as workers. But the division of labour within the workplace is consciously planned by the boss. He doesn't just hope that there are raw materials for you to work on somewhere out there. He makes sure they are stored up ready for you before you get in. And he makes sure there's a worker in place to do what's needed. All this is done in advance. He may say markets are wonderful, but he's not so stupid as to rely on them himself if he can help it.

But the only way he can make money is by selling into the marketplace. And here nothing is done in advance. You lay out your stall and hope someone wants your stuff. If they don't, then all your work has gone to waste. But you only find out after the event. The real secret of capitalist production is to be found in the factory, in the exploitation of the working class. This fact is masked by the apparent dominance of market forces over capitalist society. Marx had to start with the commodity (goods made for the market) because the market dominates the form of appearance of the capitalist economy.

Supply and demand?

"The market is governed by the forces of supply and demand". Isn't this true? Well, yes and no. Capitalism is an unplanned, anarchic, system. It is not chaos. There are forces at work to establish the 'proportional division of labour' that must exist in any society. These forces work in anarchy and through anarchy. Their immediate triggers are greed and stupidity. Capitalists all search for a higher rate of profit. Those on the ball enough will spot a shortage by raising prices. By moving capital into an area with high prices and an above average rate of profit they will help to eliminate the shortage. By their restless search for above-average profits, they will unconsciously help to establish an average overall rate of profit.

The apparently random fluctuations in price given by supply and demand no more contradict the role of value as the central regulator of the system than the movement of waves up and down on the surface denies the concept of sea level—which does go up and down according to the pull of the tides. Supply and demand, as Marx pointed out is just the executor of the laws of capitalism. The law of value gives us the basic structure and dynamics of the system. It is the way labour is allotted to various tasks in an unplanned system. Capitalism produces Mars bars and Coca-Cola. It also produces workers and capitalists, rich and poor, and continually reproduces these class relations through the market mechanism, driven by the law of value. The apologists of the capitalist economy say that markets give us "consumer sovereignty". The market system is in effect a giant economic democracy, where we vote with our money for what we want, not just once every five years but every time you go down the road for a bottle of milk. Consumers weigh up what goods they want most. For their part producers have to give people what they want in the quantities they want. Otherwise they go out of business.

Is this right? Neo-classical economics starts with people's wants. But where do they come from? Are they just 'exogenously given', as they say in the textbooks? Most of our wants are provided by the possibilities for humans given by the development of the productive system. It is quite likely that medieval peasants were bored on long winter nights. It is unlikely that they sat around wishing someone would hurry up and invent television. And the idea that these days giant oligopoly firms make their money by "giving people what they want" is quaint, but naive. On the contrary they spend vast sums making sure we will want what they give us, by manipulating people's wants. The most obvious way they do this is through advertising and the sales effort. This doesn't come cheap. Ten years ago advertising alone swallowed up 1.3% of our National Income. Marketing expenses also include finance credit, accounting, lawyers' fees, accounting costs, packaging, commissions, coupons, samples and trade allowances. For toiletries marketing is 14p for every £1 of sales, for soap 10p and for pharmaceuticals 8p. So much for giving people what they want!

Nor is it true that markets equate the costs and benefits to society of production for people's needs. First under capitalism production is for profit, not for need. It is just a nuisance for the capitalist that he has to sell his goods to somebody before he can realise the profit. For the system as a whole it's not a nuisance—it's a contradiction. Each capitalist strives to drive down the living standards of his workforce in order to maximise profits. But for the capitalist system the working class are their consumers. That means they should have plenty of money jangling in their pockets. One way a capitalist nation can solve this contradiction is by driving down wages at home and selling abroad. As Keynes told the MacMillan Committee during the Great Depression, "If you are part of an international system, you can always improve matters by cutting wages more than your neighbour". But for world capitalism there is no abroad. Attempts to offload the contradiction merely generalise the crisis and produce results such as the 1929 Depression.

And markets measure the costs and benefits, not to society as a whole, but for the capitalist. This can have perverse results, results that are very costly for "society", for the rest of us, but not for the capitalist firm The firm belches out smoke and pollutes our air. It does so because this is cheaper than attaching a filter. The firm doesn't have to pay the costs of hospitalisation and early death of workers with lung and respiratory illness caused by pollution. And once it's in the air, you can't 'choose' not to "consume" the pollution. Paradoxically this affects the 'consumer sovereignty' of everyone. Even a millionaire in Mexico City can't buy clean air, despite the fact that the pollution poisoning his lungs is the source of his profits.

And what sort of electoral system is it that gives 257 billionaires more "votes" (more money) than 2 billion poor people in the world? For capitalist economists the distribution of income, like wants, are 'exogenously given'. In fact capitalism produces rich and poor as inexorably as it produces Coca-Cola. But capitalism rests on the exploitation of the working class, whether organised by bureaucrats in a corporation plan (big companies have five year plans just like Stalin) or whether imposed by the apparently impersonal workings of the world market.

Having dealt with how the allocation of social labour time takes the form of value in an exchange economy it is time to look at the central mystery of the market, the ratio of exchange, or in Marxist terms the substance and magnitude of value. In *Capital* Marx starts with the isolated act of exchange of one commodity for another, in this case of twenty yards of linen for a coat. As inhabitants of a market economy, we don't blink at this notion. But what's really happening? Coats do not really confront piles of linen. People confront each other, but they do so via the products of their labour. That is why market forces are important to us, but also mystifying. Relations between people appear to us as relations between things. This is what Marx called commodity fetishism.

Value

Even in 1867 coats v linen was a tedious example, but note what else is unusual about it. In a market economy we do not usually exchange things we've produced but do not want for things we haven't produced but do want. We swap things around with money. But Marx does not want to take money for granted, as capitalist economists invariably do. He wants to show how the universal equivalent emerges inevitably as exchange becomes generalised. Like him, we will derive the money form from the value form. This belongs a little later. Since twenty yards of linen is being exchanged for a coat, they must have something in common. Clearly this cannot be a physical characteristic. Bourgeois economics argues that they are both objects of utility. But if artisans produce coats all day, they are not producing for themselves and selling the surplus. They are producing the coat for sale from the word go. In other words the coat has no utility for its maker. Sure, if nobody wants to buy it will turn out to have no exchange value. Use-value is a precondition for the determination of value. It does not determine its magnitude. Modern neo-classical economics makes marginal utility the foundation of its value theory. They obviously came up against the objection at a very early stage that water, the most vital requirement of life, is virtually free, while diamonds (basically useless lumps of carbon) are very expensive. They propound a grand "paradox of value" to be found in almost all the textbooks. This states that the reason we don't rate water very highly is because there's a lot of it about. Though water is valuable in absolute terms we don't care much for any more because we've already got a lot. We value the marginal unit, not the mass. Now really this amounts to nothing more than noticing that water is relatively abundant. Likewise diamonds are dear because they are scarce. They don't really need to go on and on about marginal utility at all. This is not good enough! Marx, and Ricardo before him, were aware that paintings by Van Gogh and the like were exceptions to the law of value. Since they are unique, they are not reproducible at will. In that case their price will be determined entirely by how much collectors are prepared to pay for them, by their utility.

But both Marx and Ricardo were concerned to analyse the production process as the life process of society. If we want to understand the social division of labour imposed by the market, we need to understand how an expansion of demand calls forth a capital inflow and an increase in the supply of the vast bulk of goods that can be increased in quantity by human effort. That bourgeois economists spend so much time contemplating the situation of people seated beside abundant springs or dying of thirst in the desert only shows how remote they are from the real production process.

Use-value and Exchange value

That a commodity is both a use-value and an exchange value is a contradiction. What does that mean? It means that labour expended on the commodity is only a potential value. Someone must be prepared to buy it. Value has to be validated in the marketplace. Likewise it is irrelevant to me if you spent twice as long to make a chair as everybody else. You have just wasted your time. I and every other buyer expect an average price determined by the extant productivity in that sector at the moment. It is not the amount of labour individually or accidentally expended on a commodity that determines value, but the amount socially necessary for its production. This is a vital concept when we come to look at the dynamics of the capitalist system.

The only thing both commodities have in common is that they are both objects of human labour. Obviously all real labour is the labour of particular types of worker, whether maker of coats or bus driver. As such they are examples of individual labour. They are also all taken from the general pool of social labour available to satisfy our needs. The worker in Malaysia is qualified to be a teacher, but capitalism in Malaysia doesn't need him as a teacher. He gets a job on the dredger digging up tin ore.

In the act of exchange social labour is seen as its opposite, social labour and concrete labour of a particular kind as representative of its opposite, abstract labour. How can the labour objectified by a worker on a dredger into tin ore be equated with the labour of a seamstress objectified in a dress? "Indifference towards specific labours corresponds to a form of society in which individuals can with ease transfer from one labour to another, and where the specific kind is a matter of chance for them, hence of indifference. Not only the category, labour, but labour in reality has here become the means of creating wealth in general, and has ceased to be organically linked with particular individuals in any specific form. Such a state of affairs is at its most developed in the most modern form of existence of modern society." (Marx - *Grundrisse*) In other words, both forms of individual, concrete labour are part of the pool of social labour available to meet our needs.

What are we doing when we use twenty yards of linen to measure the value of a coat? In effect the twenty yards of linen is used as what he called the equivalent form. In other words it is being used in a one-off act of exchange as performing one of the functions of money. A commodity is both a useful object, a use-value, and an exchange value. It contains a contradiction within itself. When it enters into exchange, the use-value of the equivalent serves to measure the exchange value of the other. The contradiction is not eliminated, it is reproduced on a higher level in the money form.

This is exactly what we do when we weigh things. We know both the things we want to compare are completely unlike in every respect but one. To be comparable, they must have some common property. They both have weight (mass). There is no such thing as weight that we can isolate and measure independently of objects with weight. Likewise with value we can't just add up the quantities of labour congealed in the product at different stages of production. In the case of weighing something we start off by placing one object on a set of scales and finding it equal to the item on the other side, say a lump of metal. At a later stage, as we start weighing things regularly, we will probably ascribe a conventional measure to the lump of metal (for example ten kilograms). This, of course, is how money emerged from the exchange process.

What we are doing in assessing value is essentially the same. First we know both commodities are products of the pool of social labour. So they have this common substance. Now let's move away from Marx's example and go with ten biros equals one pint of beer (both cost £2). Why? Marx's example might give the impression that artisans made the commodities from scratch - herded the sheep, carded the wool, tailored the coat. In that case you might think the artisans could say to themselves, "this coat contains X hours of my work." This was never Marx's intention. He was not analysing petty production—he was examining the commodity as a first step in the critique of capitalist production. Now in the case of our more recent example it should be evident that even a 20p ballpoint pen is the product of a world division of labour. And it is the product of large-scale capitalist production. The plastic is manufactured by enormous ethylene crackers by oil that has first been to a refinery. The crude oil may come from the North Sea, extracted by derricks twice the size of Nelson's column. Or it may come from the Gulf states, or Mexico, or Nigeria, or Brunei or anywhere else. We don't know. The metal tip—where does that come from? How much time did it take to extract the ore, refine the metal and shape the tip? It is overwhelmingly obvious that we cannot possibly work out how much labour time is involved in the production of even such a simple object as a cheap pen. Marx's value theory is often presented as a simple costs of production theory, where we add up labour value-added in the various stages of production to come up with a final value. Actually Adam Smith's value theory was one where he tried to assess the "contribution" of each "factor of production" to the value of the final product. Ricardo and Marx, on the other hand, resolved the value of a commodity into congealed labour time and then examined the struggle of the classes claiming to personify the factors of production over the value produced.

Just as we don't know how much weight an item has except by comparing it with something else, so we can't assess value except by comparison made in exchange. Exchange value is the phenomenal form of value. And the value of commodities is determined by the labour time socially necessary for their production.

The Dynamics of Capitalism

Why do we need a theory of value? How does it help us analyse the dynamics of capitalist society? Here's an example. The first ballpoint pen was produced by the Reynolds International Pen Company in 1945. As is usual in capitalist innovation, Reynolds did not invent the ballpoint. He just bought the patent off the shelf. The price was set at $12.50 but the cost of production was just 80c. The novelty value of the pens caught on and production, and profits, expanded sharply. Rivals cashed in, with Eversharp and Schaeffer both marketing pens at $15. By now Reynolds had pioneered mass production methods and unit costs had fallen to 60c. The cosy relationship with Schaeffer, Eversharp and Reynolds not treading on each other's toes came to an end as the Ball-point pen Company of Hollywood marketed a $9.95 model and David Kahn announced plans for the $3 pen. Reynolds retaliated with a $3.85 ballpoint, though production costs were now about 30c a go. By Christmas 1946 there were 100 manufacturers, some selling pens for $2.98. By February 1947 the cutting edge price was 98c and the following year saw the 39c ballpoint costing just 10c to mass-produce. In 1951 prices had fallen further to 25c as the ballpoint effectively replaced the fountain pen (remember them?) in everyday use.

Why did ballpoints get cheaper? Because it took less labour time to produce each one. That's obvious. It's equally obvious that Reynolds and his fellow capitalists were not using labour time calculations. They were just chasing a fast buck. And they decided, in competing with one another, that the best way to sell things cheaper than the opposition is to make them cheaper - that is with a smaller expenditure of labour time. That is precisely how the law of value asserts itself behind the backs of the individual actors.

Big business

Every year the *Financial Times* publishes its "Global 500", its list of the biggest companies in the world. Businesses are ranked by market capitalisation, which basically means total share price. In 2001 the biggest firm was General Electric (not to be confused with the British-owned General Electric Corporation). General Electric is a conglomerate with a finger in all sorts of pies—though not, these days, electricity. Its market capitalisation comes to $474,955 million. Its sales were $110,832 million, but profits were higher than Microsoft's at $15,942 million. Capital employed was again greater at $119,198 million. In many ways General Electric is more typical of the biggest business. It employs 340,000 workers. In fact if you were to rank big business by the number of workers Wal-Mart would come top with 1,140,000 on the payroll.

Jack Welch was the Chief Executive Officer of General Electric till he retired last year. He must have worked very hard. He collected $40 million in remuneration in 1997. Jack therefore got 1,400 times as much as the average blue-collar GE worker in the US. One reason the firm gave him so much is that he saved the owners (the shareholders) lots of money. He saved money by sacking loyal American operatives and 'downsizing' work to Mexico. Jack earned 9,571 times as much as the average Mexican employee. But don't get the idea Jack is basically on a wage. Most of his wedge came from stock options - the right to buy the company's shares. In the roaring stock market of the 1990s it was a one-way bet for the rich. Chief Executive Officers got 85 times as much as the rest of the workforce in 1990. By 1999 it was 475 times as much, and stock options were the crowbar opening up the gap between rich and poor. In 1979 the top 1% were hanging on to 20.5% of American income. Twenty years later it's over 40%.

In 2000 the biggest firm was Microsoft, with a market capitalisation of $586,196 million. That is nearly $600 billion! Microsoft's turnover (sales) was $19,747 million in 1999. Its pre-tax profit was $11,891 million. The figure for capital employed was $24,438 million. It should be explained that share capitalisation is an assessment of expected future profitability of the company, for that is what speculators are interested in when they buy the shares. It is not a stocktake of the assets. Most of the assets of Microsoft are in any case intangible. They are monopoly rights to intellectual property, like the Windows system itself, rights jealously guarded by high-paid lawyers. Microsoft employs 'only' 31,000 workers—though readers who know how the firm operates realise that plenty more are subcontracted into the global "team".

The great question of our age is how these gigantic corporations got rich and stay rich at the expense of the rest of us. That question is answered by Marxist economics. Let's first look at classes in capitalist society. We'll use the definitions in the *Communist Manifesto*. Our enemy is the bourgeoisie "the class of modern capitalists, owners of the means of social production and employers of wage labour." These days the means of production are owned in the form of shares. Even Bill Gates, the world's richest man, is not the sole owner of Microsoft, though he is reckoned to have a controlling interest in the company. But General Electric is more typical in this respect. No one shareholder owns more than a tiny fraction of the total stock—remember we're talking about almost $500 billion. What does this show? It shows how capital has accumulated. Big business has grown enormously since the time of Marx, when most firms were family-owned.

Classes in Capitalist Society

Then there's us. "By proletariat" (we mean) "the class of modern wage-labourers who, having no means of production of their own, are reduced to selling their labour power in order to live." Why? In 1817, at the dawn of the capitalist era, the Tory parson Townsend put it this way, "Legal constraint (to labour) is attended with too much trouble, violence and noise... whereas hunger is not only a peaceable, silent, unremitted pressure but, as the most natural motive to industry and labour, it calls forth the most powerful exertions." We work for them because it's the only way we can make a living.

OK, so owning the means of production means owning shares. It follows that owning no means of production means owning no shares. Is that right? Not quite. It's actually quite hard to be a worker in Britain these days without owning shares—directly or indirectly. The state pension has been and is being progressively run down by governments both Labour and Tory. If you're not in a company scheme and you can afford it, you'll probably feel the need to sign up to a Personal Pension Plan. In this mysterious financial institution the investment fund manager will muck around with ouija boards or throw darts at the shares pages of the *Financial Times*—and buy shares for you. If you're part of a company scheme they'll also have an investment fund manager who'll do the same. If you need insurance, or feel you want to save up for any other reason, your money will probably end up being lobbed at the Stock Exchange in some form.

With all the privatisation share give-aways under the Tories there are millions of workers with a few BT shares tucked behind the clock on the mantelpiece. They're not capitalists. They're just the sort of people who pick up fivers [five pound notes] when they see them lying on the pavement, that's all. So you can't really get away from holding shares. But you're only a capitalist if you make most of your money for owning a share in the means of production. And however you stretch the definition that's a tiny proportion of the population. Even if you include all their hangers-on the ruling class is no more than 10% of the people. The rest of us are all on the other side. It's time we all realised it! There are other classes whose interests are discussed in the *Manifesto.* But capitalist and worker are the polar classes slugging it out for control to decide what sort of economic system rules our globe for future generations.

Marx and Engels mention the middle class, "The lower strata of the middle class—the small tradespeople generally, the handicraftsmen and peasants—all these sink gradually into the proletariat, partly because their diminutive capital does not suffice for the scale on which modern industry is carried on, and is swamped in competition with the large capitalists, partly because their specialised skill is rendered worthless by new methods of production." This is one of the dazzling predictions from a document over 150 years old (the *Communist Manifesto*). This middle class heavily outnumbered the workers in all countries (with the possible exception of Britain) in 1848, Since then they have been progressively destroyed by the advance of large-scale capitalist production first in manufacturing, then in their last hide-outs of peasant agriculture and retail shops. Worker and capitalist are the polar classes in modern society, because we work, because we have to make a living—we do not own the means of production. Our oppressors do no work because they make a very good living at our expense. The middle class in Marx's sense own their own petty means of production and, like us, they have to work. When the common market was set up forty years ago 30% of the population of most European countries were peasants. They owned their own farms and worked the land themselves. Now this class has virtually disappeared all over the continent. The modern use of the phrase middle class really means middle layers. Marx was not talking about people who try to live colour-supplement life styles. But, people like university lecturers (who fifty years ago would definitely have described themselves as middle class) make a living by working for a wage Since they are workers, their employers have been as concerned as their private sector equivalents to cut wage costs and, the formerly privileged position of professionals like them has been eroded as a result. The inevitable result of these attacks has been for such people increasingly to identify themselves as working class. The great trend of the past 150 years has been a proletarianisation of these intermediate layers.

The capitalist class maintains their hold over us through their ownership of the means of production. The factories and offices where we have to earn our daily bread are in their hands. Previous ruling classes in history have also perpetuated their dominance through a collective monopoly of the means of production. In the Middle Ages the feudal lords owned the land. Further back the slaveholders owned slaves, who did all the hard work. Capitalists start with money. But in a market economy money is wealth and allows its owner to buy arcane pieces of paper which represent titles of ownership to the means of production. We are different too. As workers for a wage we are free. We can collect our cards and quit working for one capitalist but we can't give up working for them as a class. Social security levels in all capitalist countries are carefully crafted so as not to provide us with a standard of living we regard as normal. In any case they won't let you just chuck your job in and go on the dole.

Exploitation

Workers are exploited under capitalism. But how? What does this mean? The law of value analyses the circulation of commodities as an exchange of equivalents. Marx poses the problem this way (*Capital* Vol. 1) "The transformation of money into capital is to be explained... in such a way that the starting point is an exchange of equivalents. Mr. Moneybags, who is as yet only an embryo capitalist, must buy his commodities at their value and must sell them at their value; and nevertheless at the end of the process he must draw more value out of circulation than he puts into it at starting... This is the nut we have to crack!"

Nothing could be simpler than to explain the profits of the capitalist in terms of them adding a bit on the price for themselves. And capitalists like the ballpoint magnate Reynolds probably did operate with the notion of a standard mark-up. However Reynolds and the other market leaders had to drastically revise their notion of what that mark-up might be as they were confronted with the prospect of a full-scale price war in the 1940s, as the technology for producing ballpoints became standardised. Capitalists continually try to rip each other and the working class off by pushing up their prices, and therefore their profits. But first they come up against limits imposed by the law of value, the regulator of their system. Secondly marking-up prices is quite simply a zero-sum game for the boss class as a whole. What one gains, the other loses. It just cannot explain the steady unremitting flow of new income into the pockets of the rich, as they sit at home and wait for the dividends to plop on to their door-mats.

The historic dispossession of the ancestors of the modern working class, such as peasants and artisans, from their means of making a living gives the capitalists the whip hand. Marx goes on, "If, then, the owner of money is to transform his money into capital, he must find in the commodity market a free worker, free in a double sense. The worker must be able to dispose of his labour power as his own commodity; and, on the other hand he must have no other commodities for sale, must be 'free' from everything that is essential for the realisation of his labour power."

Labour Power

What is all this about labour power? We have all been led to believe we are paid for the work we put in. After all, if we work overtime or weekends, we expect to get paid more. If we're put on short time or laid off, we expect to lose money. Some of us are on piece work, where what's in our pay packet is directly linked to the effort we put in. That's certainly the way it looks. We'll be investigating the wages form later on. But Marx's discovery was that capitalists don't buy a determinate lump of work done. What they buy is a capacity, and they have to sweat the most out of it they can. Modern bourgeois economists use an efficiency wage theory to explain why some workers are paid more than the minimum market rate. It's because the bosses want to hang on to scarce skills. In turn workers may accord the firm some loyalty and commitment if they think they have a secure future there. Efficiency wage theory accepts that what the boss is getting is a capacity. It also argues that productivity can depend on the wage level paid. This turns neo-classical theory (which attempts to relate wages to productivity, so "we get paid what we're worth") completely on its head.

Marx explains, "I use the term labour power or capacity for labour, to denote the aggregate of those bodily and mental capabilities existing in a human being, which he exercises whenever he produces a use-value of any kind"... "The value of labour power, like that of every other commodity, is determined by the labour time necessary for the production, and consequently for the reproduction as well, of this specific article as well. In so far as it has value, labour power itself represents nothing more than a definite amount of average social labour which has been incorporated in it. Labour power only exists as a capacity of a living individual; its production presupposed his existence; and therefore the production of labour is dependent upon the worker's reproduction of himself, upon the worker's maintenance."

What the worker is being paid for is not the work he or she does. It is his/her keep. In a market economy everything is swapped around with money. The capitalist comes along with money hires the worker and puts her to work. He can do this because the worker has no independent access to the means of production, owned by the capitalist class as a whole. The worker is paid a sum of money, enough to keep body and soul together at whatever had become the normal standard of living for workers in that society. For workers in an advanced capitalist country that standard might be quite high by historic standards—a nice house full of electronic kit, a car in the driveway and a freezer full of food. But however much living standards may have improved over time and in the course of struggle, the gap between workers and capitalists in the age of Bill Gates is more than it ever was before. Workers will hang on to that standard of life only so long as they hold on to that job with the capitalists, in so doing providing the latter with a never-ending stream of unearned income.

The value of labour embodied in the product of our labour and the value of the labour power, the worker's subsistence, are two different things. Imagine a farmer who keeps a horse to plough a field and sow oats. The farmer feeds the horse some of the oats and sells the rest. It would be pointless for the farmer to keep a horse if it only ploughed up enough soil to feed itself. Horses have traditionally been used in agriculture because they can provide farmers with a surplus above their own subsistence. That is also why capitalists employ workers. It's easy to see what's happening in the case of the horse; you can actually divide a crop up into oats for subsistence and oats for sale. It's more difficult with the worker. The worker comes in to produce commodities, which very often are consumed neither by labourers or capitalists. The commodities are sold on the open market. The worker is paid off with a wage, which he or she is free to spend as he/she thinks fit. That's the theory. Really you have to pay the rent, and you have to eat. By the time you've paid out on essentials all you have left is pocket money. Meanwhile the boss trousers the surplus left over in money form.

The worker adds value in the process of production. That is a well recognised fact. The Inland Revenue can compute value added in order to calculate how much VAT they should be getting. This product of the worker's labour undergoes a two way split. If we look at every day, every hour, every minute of time or every piece of work done value added can be divided in two. Marx called these necessary and surplus labour. Necessary labour is what goes to maintain the workers' labour power—it is paid labour and goes towards the workers' wage. Surplus labour is labour which goes to keep not just your immediate boss, but the whole class of hangers on, in idleness. This is unpaid labour.

Hostile commentators often attribute to Marx the notion that workers could only ever get an absolute subsistence minimum wage. This, of course, is the prelude to "proving" that Marx was wrong, or at least completely out of date. Actually Marx and Engels were scornful of contemporary theories of the "iron law of wages" as was put forward by Lassalle, an opponent of theirs in the German labour movement. Quite logically Lassalle contested that, since wages were fixed, trade union activity and strikes were a waste of time. Marx, as head of the International Working Men's Association, vigorously argued the opposite. The International actually spent most of its time and effort raising funds for workers on strike and issuing leaflets in different languages and appeals against the danger of international scabbing. Marx was also one of the nineteenth century economists most aware of rising standards of living for the workers.

Moreover he saw these early faltering steps of the labour movement in gaining an improved standard of living through struggle as the necessary first stage in the process of self-emancipation of the working class. "The comprehensiveness of what are called 'needs', and the method of their satisfaction, are likewise historical products, depending upon the stage of civilisation a country has reached; and depending, moreover, to a very considerable extent upon what conditions, and therefore with what habits and claims, the class of free workers has come into existence. Thus the value of labour power includes... a historical and a moral factor."

The division of the working time into paid and unpaid labour is not a feature of capitalism alone. All ruling classes in history have maintained themselves by exploiting the oppressed class. "Surplus labour was not a new discovery made by capital. Wherever a part of society has a monopoly of the means of production the worker, whether free or bond, must supplement the labour time necessary for his own maintenance by surplus labour time in which he produces the means of subsistence for the owner of the means of production, whether this owner be an Athenian devotee of the Good and the Beautiful, an Etruscan theocrat, a Roman citizen, a Norman baron, an American slave owner, a Wallachian boyar, a modern landlord or a capitalist."

The difference is that, under capitalism, exploitation is not obvious. Under feudalism the peasants often worked three days on their own strips of land and three days on the lord's land. The product of the first three days' work would be consumed in the peasant household while the product of the next three days labour was harvested and taken to the castle for the lord and his retainers. Whatever the contemporary religious or traditional justification of this practice, it would not have been necessary for medieval revolutionaries to have written erudite tomes explaining that this was exploitation. Likewise with the slave. Actually it would seem here that all the slave's labour was unpaid. In fact if the slave was producing a commercial crop such as cotton or tobacco, the slave owner would have to put aside a part of his revenue to buy food for the slaves. The same division of the product of work into paid and unpaid portion takes place in all forms of class society.

The reality of exploitation under capitalism is complicated by several other factors. First the medieval peasant is likely to harvest a crop with his own hands. It is obvious that the food he eats is the fruit of his own labour. Under capitalism there is a division of labour within the workplace as well as the division of labour imposed by production for the market. No one worker can point to the product and say 'this is mine'. A commodity such as a mass-produced car passes through the hands of hundreds of detail workers. It is the product of the collective labour of the factory 'hands'. This is a broader concept than just assembly-line workers. A big factory is likely to hire separate cleaning staff. The alternative, of course, would be to stop work while the production line workers clean up. Likewise the Coventry toolroom agreement recognises maintenance engineers as productive workers by cutting them in on any bonuses or piece work agreements.

Secondly the surplus is not all consumed by your direct employer. Marxists have used the formula—rent, interest and profit—to explain the division of surplus value among the different fractions of the capitalist. Actually it's even more complicated than that, as we shall see. But if the banks raise interest rates or industrial rents go up, that will hit the industrialist's profits quite independently of the struggle of the workers for higher wages, for a bigger share of what they produce.

Finally the capitalist has other costs than labour. For a modern multinational, wages may represent no more than 5-10% of total costs. Though the value added by the worker may be divided into necessary and surplus labour, the value of the commodity comes in three parts. There is surplus value, the unpaid labour of the working class that the capitalists all feed off. Then there is the time put in by the worker to reproduce the elements of his or her own wages. When the capitalist 'advances' this to the worker in the form of a wage, Marx calls this variable capital. It is variable because it is part of the money capital, which is capable of yielding a surplus in the process of production. All the other outlays by the boss, for raw materials, machinery heating light and power, and so on, are called constant capital by Marx. These are called constant capital because they pass their value unchanged to the final product. They contain surplus value from workers further down the chain of production.

This is easy to see in the case of raw materials. Nobody thinks that the chocolate coating to a sweet adds any value apart from its cost for the capitalist who buys it. Machinery does aid the productivity of labour but does not itself add value. To take the simplest case, the capitalists (or rather their managers) know a machine will produce one million widgets over a ten year period, by which time it will be clapped out. If the machine costs £1 million they will assess the depreciation on the machine embodied in each widget at £1. So if they put £1 aside every time they sell a widget they will have £1 million when it's time to buy a new machine. In practice capitalists will have to take account of the fact that the machine will probably be obsolescent and have to be scrapped before it is physically worn out, but the principle is clear. Machinery just passes its value unchanged to the final product to the extent that it depreciates. It aids the worker in creating surplus value but does not itself create new value. That is why all the other elements of the production process apart from labour power count for the capitalist as constant capital.

Exploitation in Action

Let's look at exploitation in practice. Figures come from the research department of the American textile workers' union, UNITE. If an American woman spends $100 on a dress:-

$54 goes to the shop. But all the retailer does is pass the goods along and hang them up for people to look at. Where does the money come from? The sales effort squanders huge resources in modern capitalism. These resources can only come from the surplus value generated in the productive part of the economy.

$18 goes on materials. The manufacturing firm just buys these in.

$16 is manufacturing overheads and profit. This is a tricky one to analyse in Marxist terms. Heating and lighting are costs, just like fabrics and zip fasteners. But some of the 'costs' will really be a share of the profits. Rent, for instance, is really siphoned off by another section of the property owning class. To keep it simple, we'll assume that $15 of those $16 really are costs and the poor old manufacturer only makes $1 on a $100 dress (a rate of profit of just 1%).

The worker who makes the dress gets $12 back in wages.

Now let's look at this in Marxist terms:-

Constant capital is $33 - $18 for materials, $15 for other production costs.

Variable capital is $12

Surplus value is $55, of which $1 goes to the immediate boss and $54 on Oxford Street rents and the pay of salespeople, who no doubt work very hard, but do not generate new values through their work.

The rate of surplus value or rate of exploitation is the amount of time the worker puts in to reproduce the elements of her wages compared with the amount of time the worker devotes to enriching the capitalist class. In this case the rate of exploitation is more than 450%!

Here's how the rich get rich and the poor stay poor. And it's true whether you work on a farm or in a factory, and whether you dish up burgers or write computer programmes. The rich get rich off our unpaid labour.

Don't you think a rate of exploitation of 450% is good enough for the bosses? Don't you think they'd be happy getting a worker to put in about 11 minutes every hour to get his or her wages back while he/she works the other 49 minutes to keep the capitalist class in clover? Not on your nelly! It's never enough. There is a compulsion on individual capitalists to squeeze more and more out of you. In part the whip is supplied by competition with other firms. If you have to beat the opposition, the best way is to sell the stuff cheaper. The best way to sell cheaper is to make it cheaper—that is with less labour. They call it cutting costs, but that's what it is. Let's see what this race does for the development of the system as a whole.

The bosses are always out to get that little bit more out of the workers. One obvious way they do that is to get you to work longer hours. Let's stick with the garment industry.

Lina Rodriguez Meza, a clothing worker in New York explains. "When it's busy, we work up to sixty to sixty-three hours. The conditions in the factory are not good. In the factory where I work, almost everyone is from Ecuador. Those people work hard. And since they come very far from their land, they come and are afraid of losing their jobs, so they enslave themselves."

Lina's in a difficult position. Nobody wants to put in over sixty hours in a week. But the basic rate is so low. And in the fashion industry work is completely casual, as she explains. "Last week we only worked for fifteen hours. And now we worked two days in a row, but it seems like we're going to be off again."

Lina actually needs the overtime to make ends meet. She is a worker in the richest country in the world.

What's going on here? As we have seen, there is a compulsion on the capitalist class to try to get more and more out of us, to raise the rate of exploitation. One way to do this is what Marx called the extraction of absolute surplus value. This means exploiting the worker over a longer time. For instance if a worker does four hours to earn their keep and then puts in another four hours to help the boss out, the rate of exploitation is 100%. But if the worker can be induced to slave for ten hours a day, then that extra two hours is a free lunch for their boss. In Marx's time the capitalists just used their class power to lengthen the working day. Since workers were usually paid by the day, the struggle over the length of the working day was a basic form of class struggle.

Critics of Marx say that's all out of date. What is happening to Lina and millions like her shows that the extraction of absolute surplus value is still a very effective way of lining the bosses' pockets. That's why it's still going on in the new millennium—in the heart of New York. We all know the jobs—security guards, caterers, cleaners, drivers, railway workers—where it's understood that you'll have to work overtime to make enough to feed a family on because the basic rate is so low.

Most workers in the United States and the other rich countries did gain better wages and conditions—for a time. They did it by organising in trade unions and threatening the strike weapon. Any strike shows that when the workers stop working, nothing gets done. It's us that produce the wealth.

But now big business is trying to take back all the gains of past struggles. Why?—because they can. Because they can roam the world looking for cheap labour to exploit. Because they can sniff out and batten on to low pay pockets in rich countries. Because if they can use child labour, they will use child labour. Because if they can use slave labour, they will use slave labour.

How does all this affect workers in rich countries such as the United States. In 1973 there were nearly 1.5 million clothing and textile workers in the USA. Some of them have lost their jobs as firms like Nike pull up stakes and go where they can get away with paying workers less. While only 4% of clothing was imported into the States in the 1960s, it's now gone up to 60%.

But 860,000 still work in the rag trade in the United States. American bosses have responded to foreign competition in different ways. One response of textile and clothing companies in the rich countries to foreign competitors has been to make sure that, if they're paying you more than workers in Pakistan or El Salvador, they get more out of you.

Relative Surplus Value

American clothing bosses have cut costs by mechanising. Whereas only 6% of clothing production in the United States used modern machinery in the 1960s, twenty years later the business was 40% automated. As a result productivity in clothing manufacture has doubled in the rich countries over a twenty year period. In other words workers are producing twice as much as they did before. As a result they are working less time to make up the value of their wages and more time for the boss class. This is what Marx called the production of relative surplus value. Relative surplus value can be increased by raising the intensity of labour (which is what bosses were trying to do to British textile workers in the 1930s—as we see below) or by raising the productivity of labour through mechanisation.

What has happened to American workers' wages as a result of mechanisation? Clothing workers' wages in the USA buy exactly the same as they did twenty years ago. The entire benefits of this increased productivity has gone to the clothing employers.

What's this all about? We know that a simple and obvious way of raising the rate of exploitation when the labour movement is weak is to make the workers put in more hours to extract more absolute surplus value. Marx showed how this strategy came up against the resistance of the working class in the cotton textile industry in the middle of the nineteenth century. The workers imposed their own limits through strike action and later won a legal limit on the working day. If capitalists can't increase hours without limits to raise the rate of exploitation then they're going to have to make the workers achieve more in the hours when they do have them at their disposal. If a worker is knocking out twice as many dresses in eight hours, then they're reproducing the elements of their wages in two hours instead of four. That leaves six hours for the production of surplus value.

One way of extracting relative surplus value is by raising the productivity of labour. This usually involves the accumulation of capital with more and more machinery behind the elbow of each worker.

Intensification of Labour

Another way is by raising the intensity of labour. If you can't lengthen hours, then they make sure they get more out of you while you're there. Two classic ways of getting more sweat out of workers are speeding up the track and getting the workers to mind more machines.

This has been going on a long time. However much you produce for them they always want more. At the time of the great depression of 1929-33, the British cotton capitalists thought it was a good time to put the boot in to textile workers. They demanded that weavers mind six looms instead of four—like Japanese workers. The "more-looms" dispute, went together with a demand for pay cuts of up to 12 ½ %—more work for less pay! This triggered a walkout of 150,000 weavers in Lancashire. After a bitter dispute in which police baton charges against picket lines became routine, the strike was sold out by the trade union tops.

The process whereby more and more dead labour (constant capital, in Marx's term) is used relative to living labour in the production process is called the accumulation of capital. It is the curse of the individual capitalist that they cannot just consume the unpaid labour of the working class in luxury living (though they don't do badly). They are forced by competition among themselves to plough back a major part of their ill-gotten gains. This in turn raises the productivity of labour. By accumulating capital and creating a mass working class all over the world capitalism is creating the conditions for its own supercession as a system. It is taking us to the threshold of a society of abundance. Yet at the present time half the world's population lives in desperate poverty on $2 a day or less.

The accompanying diagram adapted from the *Economist* in 1985 shows that the productivity of labour in textile spinning has gone up two thousand times since the industrial revolution began around 1750 - up to 1980. It's still rising, faster than ever. So they are certainly exploiting us more! We've deliberately used the old-fashioned example of spinning. The reader will probably have been told about the spinning jenny and the industrial revolution at school and Marx dealt with it extensively in his writings. But clearly the most spectacular starburst of productivity is to be seen in industries subject to computerisation. "The speed at which computers are capable of carrying immense computations is almost impossible to grasp. As long ago as the early 1960s, when the space-frame centrepiece of Expo 67 was being designed, a computer was employed for two hours. A mathematical graduate could have performed the same calculations, but would have taken about 30,000 years. This is equivalent to about 1000 mathematicians working for their entire lifetimes." (from Mike Cooley - *Architect and bee*).

Increasing Organic Composition of Capital

So modern textile machinery makes workers enormously more productive than people with distaffs three hundred years ago. Likewise Computer Aided Design means a three dimensional design of a complex piece of machinery can be generated in an instant - whereas twenty years ago a team of draftsmen with 5H pencils and 'T' squares took a week to do the same job. The examples can be multiplied at will. But there is a fly in the ointment. Modern textile machinery costs more than distaffs. A bank of computers costs more than pencils and 'T' squares. It costs a lot more to exploit the workers more. Dead labour progressively replaces living labour in production. Marx called the secular trend for the ratio of constant capital (outlays on plant and raw materials) to rise relative to variable capital (money laid out on wages) an increase in the organic composition of capital. And it's been going on all over. One example: General Motors opened its Saturn plant on a greenfield site in Tennessee. The plant cost $5 billion—that's $5 thousand million. It will employ about 6,000 workers. That's nearly $1 million behind the elbow of each worker in the modern car industry.

You won't stop the bosses exploiting workers. As long as they are bosses, they have to do that. But you'll never stop workers fighting back against exploitation either. As long as they are wage workers they will have to fight for a better future. That means an end to the bosses' system and the socialist transformation of society.

THE LIVING THOUGHTS OF KARL MARX BY TROTSKY (EXTRACT)

Certain of Marx's argumentations, especially in the first, the most difficult chapter, may seem to the uninitiated reader far too discursory, hair-splitting, or "metaphysical". As a matter of fact, this impression arises in consequence of the want of habit to approach overly habitual phenomena scientifically. The commodity has become such an all-pervasive, customary and familiar part of our daily existence that we, lulled to sleep, do not even attempt to consider why men relinquish important objects, needed to sustain life, in exchange for tiny discs of gold or silver that are of no earthly use whatever. The matter is not limited to the commodity. One and all of the categories (the basic concepts) of market economy seem to be accepted without analysis, as self-evident, as if they were the natural basis of human relations. Yet, while the realities of the economic process are human labour, raw materials, tools, machines, division of labour, the necessity to distribute finished products among the participants of the labour process, and the like, such categories as "commodity," "money," "wages," "capital," "profit," "tax," and the like are only semi-mystical reflections in men's heads of the various aspects of a process of economy which they do not understand and which is not under their control. To decipher them, a thoroughgoing scientific analysis is indispensable.

In the United States, where a man who owns a million is referred to as being "worth" a million, market concepts have sunk in deeper than anywhere else. Until quite recently Americans gave very little thought to the nature of economic relations. In the land of the most powerful economic system economic theory continued to be exceedingly barren. Only the present deep-going crisis of American economy has bluntly confronted public opinion with the fundamental problems of capitalist society. In any event, whoever has not overcome the habit of uncritically accepting the ready-made ideological reflections of economic development, whoever has not reasoned out, in the footsteps of Marx, the essential nature of the commodity as the basic cell of the capitalist organism, will prove to be forever incapable of scientifically comprehending the most important and the most acute manifestations of our epoch.

Marx's Method

Having established science as cognition of the objective recurrences of nature, man has tried stubbornly and persistently to exclude himself from science, reserving for himself special privileges in the shape of alleged intercourse with supersensory forces (religion), or with timeless moral precepts (idealism). Marx deprived man of these odious privileges definitely and forever, looking upon him as a natural link in the evolutionary process of material nature; upon human society as the organisation of production and distribution; upon capitalism as a stage in the development of human society.

It was not Marx's aim to discover the "eternal laws" of economy. He denied the existence of such laws. The history of the development of human society is the history of the succession of various systems of economy, each operating in accordance with its own laws. The transition from one systems to another was always determined by the growth of the productive forces, i.e., of technique and the organisation of labour. Up to a certain point, social changes are quantitative in character and do not alter the foundations of society, i.e., the prevalent forms of property. But a point is reached when the matured productive forces can no longer contain themselves within the old forms of property; then follows a radical change in the social order, accompanied by shocks. The primitive commune was either superseded or supplemented by slavery; slavery was succeeded by serfdom with its feudal superstructure; the commercial development of cities brought Europe in the sixteenth century to the capitalist order, which thereupon passed through several stages. In his *Capital*, Marx does not study economy in general, but capitalist economy, which has its own specific laws. Only in passing does he refer to the other economic systems to elucidate the characteristics of capitalism.

The self-sufficient economy of the primitive peasant family has no need of a "political economy," for it is dominated on the one hand by the forces of nature and on the other by the forces of tradition. The self-contained natural economy of the Greeks or the Romans, founded on slave labour, was ruled by the will of the slave-owner, whose "plan" in turn was directly determined by the laws of nature and routine. The same might also be said about the mediaeval estate with its peasant serfs. In all these instances economic relations were clear and transparent in their primitive crudity. But the case of contemporary society is altogether different. It destroyed the old self-contained connections and the inherited modes of labour. The new economic relations have linked cities and villages, provinces and nations. Division of labour has encompassed the planet, having shattered tradition and routine, these bonds have not composed themselves to some definite plan, but rather apart from human consciousness and foresight, and it would seem as if behind the very backs of men. The interdependence of men, groups, classes, nations, which follows from division of labour, is not directed or managed by anyone. People work for each other without knowing each other, without inquiring about one another's needs, in the hope, and even with the assurance, that their relations will somehow regulate themselves. And by and large they do, or rather were wont to.

It is utterly impossible to seek the causes for the recurrences of capitalist society in the subjective consciousness—in the intentions or plans—of its members. The objective recurrences of capitalism were formulated before science began to think about them seriously. To this day the preponderant majority of men know nothing about the laws that govern capitalist economy. The whole strength of Marx's method was in his approach to economic phenomena, not from the subjective point of view of certain persons, but from the objective point of view of society as a whole, just as an experimental natural scientist approaches a beehive or an anthill.

For economic science the decisive significance is what and how people do, not what they themselves think about their actions. At the base of society is not religion and morality, but nature and labour. Marx's method is materialistic, because it proceeds from existence to consciousness, not the other way around. Marx's method is dialectic, because it regards both nature and society as they evolve, and evolution itself as the constant struggle of conflicting forces.

Marxism and Official Science

Marx had his predecessors. Classical political economy—Adam Smith, David Ricardo—reached its full bloom before capitalism had grown old, before it began to fear the morrow. Marx paid to both great classicists the perfect tribute of profound gratitude. Nevertheless the basic error of classical economics was its view of capitalism as humanity's normal existence for all time instead of merely as one historical stage in the development of society. Marx began with a criticism of that political economy, exposed its errors, as well as the contradictions of capitalism itself, and demonstrated the inevitability of its collapse. As Rosa Luxemburg has very aptly observed, Marx's economic teaching is a child of classical economics, a child whose birth cost its mother her life.

Science does not reach its goal in the hermetically sealed study of the scholar, but in flesh-and-blood society. All the interests and passions that rend society asunder, exert their influence on the development of science—especially of political economy, the science of wealth and poverty. The struggle of workers against capitalists forced the theoreticians of the bourgeoisie to turn their backs upon a scientific analysis of the system of exploitation and to busy themselves with a bare description of economic facts, a study of the economic past and, what is immeasurably worse, a downright falsification of things as they are for the purpose of justifying the capitalist regime. The economic doctrine which is nowadays taught in official institutions of learning and preached in the bourgeois press offers no dearth of important factual material, yet it is utterly incapable of encompassing the economic process as a whole and discovering its laws and perspectives, nor has it any desire to do so. Official political economy is dead. Real knowledge of capitalist society can be obtained only through Marx's *Capital*.

Three Sources and Component Parts of Marxism by Lenin (extract)

Having recognised that the economic system is the foundation on which the political superstructure is erected, Marx devoted his greatest attention to the study of this economic system. Marx's principal work, *Capital*, is devoted to a study of the economic system of modern, i.e., capitalist, society.

Classical political economy, before Marx, evolved in England, the most developed of the capitalist countries. Adam Smith and David Ricardo, by their investigations of the economic system, laid the foundations of the *labour theory of value*. Marx continued their work; he provided a proof of the theory and developed it consistently. He showed that the value of every commodity is determined by the quantity of socially necessary labour time spent on its production.

Where the bourgeois economists saw a relation between things (the exchange of one commodity for another) Marx revealed a *relation between people*. The exchange of commodities expresses the connection between individual producers through the market. *Money* signifies that the connection is becoming closer and closer, inseparably uniting the entire economic life of the individual producers into one whole. *Capital* signifies a further development of this connection: man's labour-power becomes a commodity. The wage-worker sells his labour-power to the owner of land, factories and instruments of labour. The worker spends one part of the day covering the cost of maintaining himself and his family (wages), while the other part of the day he works without remuneration, creating for the capitalist *surplus-value*, the source of profit, the source of the wealth of the capitalist class.

The doctrine of surplus-value is the corner-stone of Marx's economic theory.

Capital, created by the labour of the worker, crushes the worker, ruining small proprietors and creating an army of unemployed. In industry, the victory of large-scale production is immediately apparent, but the same phenomenon is also to be observed in agriculture, where the superiority of large-scale capitalist agriculture is enhanced, the use of machinery increases and the peasant economy, trapped by money-capital, declines and falls into ruin under the burden of its backward technique. The decline of small-scale production assumes different forms in agriculture, but the decline itself is an indisputable fact.

By destroying small-scale production, capital leads to an increase in productivity of labour and to the creation of a monopoly position for the associations of big capitalists. Production itself becomes more and more social—hundreds of thousands and millions of workers become bound together in a regular economic organism—but the product of this collective labour is appropriated by a handful of capitalists. Anarchy of production, crises, the furious chase after markets and the insecurity of existence of the mass of the population are intensified.

By increasing the dependence of the workers on capital, the capitalist system creates the great power of united labour.

Marx traced the development of capitalism from embryonic commodity economy, from simple exchange, to its highest forms, to large-scale production.

And the experience of all capitalist countries, old and new, year by year demonstrates clearly the truth of this Marxian doctrine to increasing numbers of workers.

Capitalism has triumphed all over the world, but this triumph is only the prelude to the triumph of labour over capital.

Questions on Marxist economics

1) What are the preconditions for capitalism?
2) What is primitive accumulation?
3) What is the difference between use-value and exchange-value?
4) What is a commodity?
5) What is socially necessary labour?
6) Distinguish between abstract and concrete labour.
7) What is labour power and how is its value determined?

8) What is money and what is its function?
9) What governs the price of commodities?
10) How do the laws of supply and demand apply?
11) Can you say that the workers are robbed by the capitalist class?
12) Where does surplus value come from?
13) Why can't the circulation of capital be the source of surplus value?
14) What is absolute surplus value?
15) What is relative surplus value?
16) What is constant and variable capital?
17) What is the rate of profit and why is there a tendency for it to decline?
18) What is the historical tendency of capitalist accumulation?
19) Why does over-production occur under capitalism?
20) What are the other main contradictions of capitalism?

Suggested reading

Wage Labour and Capital, Marx
Value, Price and Profit, Marx
Capital in 3 volumes, Marx
Theories of Surplus Value, Marx
The Grundrisse, Marx
The Critique of Political Economy, Marx
On Capital, Engels
Anti-Dühring, Engels
The Three Sources and Component Parts of Marxism, Lenin
Marxism in Our Time (in The Living Thoughts of Karl Marx), Trotsky
Will there be a Slump? Ted Grant
Economic articles at Marxist.com

Obtainable from Wellred Books, PO Box 50525, London E14 6WG
Or at the online Marxist bookshop at wellred.marxist.com
An important Marxist online resouce is at marxists.org

What is Marxism?

By Alan Woods and Rob Sewell

Foreword

Marxism, or Scientific Socialism, is the name given to the body of ideas first worked out by Karl Marx (1818-1883) and Friedrich Engels (1820-1895). In their totality, these ideas provide a fully worked-out theoretical basis for the struggle of the working class to attain a higher form of human society—socialism.

While the conceptions of Marxism have been subsequently developed and enriched by the historical experience of the working class itself, the fundamental ideas remain unshaken, providing a firm foundation for the labour movement today. Neither before, nor since the lifetime of Marx and Engels have any superior, more truthful or scientific theories been advanced to explain the movement of society and the role of the working class in that movement. A knowledge of Marxism therefore equips the proletariat theoretically for the great historic task of the socialist transformation of Society.

It is this fact which explains the constant and bitter attacks on all aspects of Marxism which have been delivered by every conceivable defender of the existing social order—from the Tory to the Fabian, from the Jesuit priest to the university professor. From the very spleen of these attacks, to the fact that they have to be kept up continuously despite the fact that every single one of the pundits in turn claims to have "finally disposed" of Marxism, the thinking member of the labour movement can deduce two facts. First, that the defenders of capitalism recognise in Marxism the most dangerous challenge to their system, and thereby also instantly confess the truth in it, despite all their attempts to "disprove" it. Second, that far from disappearing under the heap of abuse, quack "exposures", and flagrant distortions, the theories of Marx and Engels are steadily gaining ground, particularly within the active layers of the labour movement, as increasing numbers of workers, under the impact of the crisis of capitalism, strive to discover the real meaning of the forces which shape their lives, in order to be able to consciously influence and determine their own destiny.

The theories of Marxism provide the thinking worker with such an understanding—a thread which is capable of leading him through the confused labyrinth of events, of the complex processes of society, of economics, of the struggle of classes, of politics. Armed with this sword the worker can cut the Gordian knot which binds him to the mightiest obstacle in the way of the advancement of himself and his class—ignorance.

It is to keep this knot firmly in place that the hired representatives of the ruling class struggle with might and main to discredit Marxism in the eyes of the working class. It is the duty of every serious worker of the labour movement to conquer for himself or herself the theories of Marx and Engels, as an essential prerequisite for the conquest of society by the working people.

Yet there are obstacles in the path of the worker's struggle for theory and understanding far more intractable than the scribblings of priests and professors. A man or woman who is obliged to toil long hours in industry, who has not had the benefit of a decent education and consequently lacks the habit of reading, finds great difficulty in absorbing some of the more complex ideas, especially at the outset. Yet it was for workers that Marx and Engels wrote, and not for "clever" students and middle class people. "Every beginning is difficult" no matter what science we are talking about. Marxism is a science and therefore makes heavy demands upon the beginner. But every worker who is active in the trade unions or Labour Party knows that nothing is worthwhile if attained without a degree of struggle and sacrifice. It is the activists in the labour movement at whom the present pamphlet is aimed. To the active worker who is prepared to persevere, one promise can be made: once the initial effort is made to come to grips with unfamiliar and new ideas, the theories of Marxism will be found to be basically straight-forward and simple. Moreover—and this should be emphasised—the worker who acquires by patient effort an understanding of Marxism will turn out to be a better theoretician than most students, just because he can grasp the ideas not merely in the abstract, but concretely, as applied to his own life and work.

All exploiting classes attempt to morally justify their class rule by portraying them, as the highest, most natural form of social development, deliberately concealing the system of exploitation by disguising and distorting the truth. The present day capitalist class, through their professional hirelings and hangers on, have elaborately evolved a whole new philosophy and morality to justify their ruling position in society.

The working class, on the contrary, has no material interest in distorting the truth, and sets itself the task of laying bare the realities of capitalism in order to consciously prepare for its emancipation. Far from seeking a special position for itself, the working class has the aim of abolishing capitalism and with it all class distinctions and privileges. To do so it must reject the outlook of the capitalists, and seek for itself a new Marxist method of understanding.

The Marxist method provides a richer, fuller, more comprehensive view of society and life in general, and clears away the veil of mysticism in understanding human and social development. Marxist philosophy explains that the driving force of history is neither "Great Men" nor the super-natural, but stems from the development of the productive forces (industry, science, technique, etc.) themselves. It is economics, in the last analysis, that determines the conditions of life, the habits and consciousness of human beings.

Each new re-organisation of society—be it slavery, feudalism or capitalism—has ushered in an enormous development of the productive forces which in turn gave men and women greater powers over nature. As soon as a social system proves unable to develop these forces of production, then that society enters an epoch of revolution. However, in the case of the change from capitalism to socialism, the process is not automatic but requires the conscious intervention of the working class to carry through this task of history. Failure to do so in the long run would pave the way for the advent of reaction and eventual world war.

Capitalism has once again entered a new world economic crisis resulting in mass unemployment on the lines of the 1930s. The quack theories of capitalist economists have proved utterly incapable of preventing recessions, which has driven the ruling class to ditch Keynesianism and re-adopt the old measures of "sound finance", of monetarism. Rather than rescue the situation this latter programme has served to deepen and prolong the crisis!

Only Marxism has been able to expose the contradictions of Capitalism which result periodically in depression and slump. Capitalism has now completely exhausted its historical role in developing the productive basis of society. Hemmed in by the nation state and private ownership, the productive forces are systematically destroyed in the face of the mass overproduction of commodities and capital.

As Marx himself explained: "In these crises there breaks out an epidemic that in all earlier epochs, would have seemed an absurdity—the epidemic of overproduction.

"Society suddenly finds itself put back into a state of monetary barbarism; it appears as if a famine, a universal war of destruction has cut off the supply of every means of subsistence; industry and commerce seem to be destroyed. And why? Because there is too much civilisation, too much means of subsistence, too much industry, too much commerce. The productive forces at the disposal of society no longer tend to further the development of the conditions of bourgeois property; on the contrary they have become too powerful for these conditions by which they are fettered, and so as soon as they overcome these fetters, they bring disorder into the whole of bourgeois society, endanger the existence of bourgeois property."

The present pamphlet brings together for the first time the three supplements of the South Wales Bulletin of Marxist Studies (first published in the 1970s) as a small contribution to the increasing thirst for the ideas of Marxism. It is also fitting that the issue of the pamphlet coincides with the centenary of Karl Marx's death, on 14 March 1883, the co-founder with Engels, of scientific socialism.

This pamphlet however is not intended to provide a complete exposition of Marxism, but to assist the worker-student in his approach to the subject by giving a rough outline of some basic ideas, plus a selected reading list with which he may continue his studies. Marx and Engels themselves wrote many brief pamphlets and shorter explanatory works aimed at popularising their theories among the working class, and these provide the basis of the suggested reading list.

The study of Marxism falls under three main headings, corresponding broadly to philosophy, social history and economics, or, to give them their correct names, Dialectical Materialism, Historical Materialism and the Labour Theory of Value. These are the famous "three component parts of Marxism" of which Lenin wrote.

18 February, 1983

DIALECTICAL MATERIALISM

What is a philosophy?

At each stage in human history, men and women have worked out some sort of picture of the world and their place in it. They develop a Philosophy. The pieces they use to make up this picture have been obtained by observing nature and through generalising their day to day experiences.

Some people believe they have no need of such a philosophy or world outlook. Yet in practise everyone has a philosophy, even if it is not consciously worked out. People who live by rule of thumb or "common sense" and think they are doing without theory, in practice think in the traditional way. Marx once said that the dominant ideas of society are those of the ruling class. To maintain and justify its rule, the capitalist class makes use of every available means to distort the consciousness of the worker. The school, church, TV, and press are used to foster the ideology of the ruling class and indoctrinate the worker into accepting their system as the most natural permanent form of society. In the absence of a conscious socialist philosophy, they accept unconsciously the capitalist one.

At each point in class society, the rising revolutionary class, aiming to change society, have to fight for a new world outlook and have to attack the old philosophy, which, being based on the old order, justified and defended it.

Idealism and materialism

Throughout the history of philosophy we find two camps, the idealist and the materialist. The common idea of "idealism" (i.e. honesty, uprightness in the pursuit of ideals) and "materialism" (i.e. base, greedy, money-grabbing egoism) has nothing to do with philosophical idealism and philosophical materialism.

Many great thinkers of the past were idealists, notably Plato and Hegel. This school of thought looks upon nature and history as a reflection of ideas or spirit. The theory that men and women and every material thing was created by a divine Spirit, is a basic concept of idealism. This outlook is expressed in a number of ways, yet its basis is that ideas govern the development of the material world. History is explained as a history of thought. People's actions are seen as resulting from abstract thoughts, and not from their material needs. Hegel went one step further, being a consistent idealist, and turned thoughts into an independent "Idea" existing outside of the brain and independent of the material world. The latter was merely a reflection of this Idea. Religion is part and parcel of philosophical idealism.

The materialist thinkers on the other hand, have maintained that the material world is real and that nature or matter is primary. The mind or ideas are a product of the brain. The brain, and therefore ideas, arose at a certain stage in the development of living matter. The basic cornerstones of Materialism are as follows:

(a) The material world, known to us by our senses and explored by science, is real. The development of the world is due to its own natural laws, without any recourse to the supernatural.

(b) There is only one world, the material one. Thought is a product of matter (the brain) without which there can be no separate ideas. Therefore minds or ideas cannot exist in isolation apart from matter. General ideas are only reflections of the material world. "To me," wrote Marx, "the idea is nothing else than the material world reflected in the human mind, and translated into forms of thought." And further, "Social being determines consciousness".

The idealists conceive of consciousness, of thought, as something external, and opposed to matter, to nature. This opposition is something entirely false and artificial. There is a close correlation between the laws of thought and the laws of nature, because the former follow and reflect the latter. Thought cannot derive its categories from itself, but only from the external world. Even the most seemingly abstract thoughts are in fact derived from the observation of the material world.

Even an apparently abstract science like pure mathematics has, in the last analysis, been derived from material reality, and is not spun from the brain. The school-child secretly counts his material fingers under a material desk before solving an abstract arithmetical problem. In so doing, he is re-creating the origins of mathematics itself. We base ourselves upon the decimal system because we have ten fingers. The Roman numerals were originally based on the representation of fingers.

According to Lenin, "this is materialism: matter acting on our sense organs produces sensation. Sensations depend upon the brain, nerves, retina, etc., i.e., matter is primary. Sensation, thought, consciousness are the supreme product of matter".

People are a part of nature, who develop their ideas in interaction with the rest of the world. Mental processes are real enough, but they are not something absolute, outside nature. They should be studied in their material and social circumstances in which they arise. "The phantoms formed in the human brain," stated Marx, "are necessarily, sublimates of their material life-process." Later he concluded, "morality, religion, metaphysics, all the rest of ideology and their corresponding forms of consciousness, thus no longer retain the semblance of independence. They have no history, no development, but men, developing their material production and their material intercourses, alter along with this their real existence their thinking and the product of their thinking. Life is not determined by consciousness, but consciousness by life."

The origins of materialism

"The original home of all modern materialism," wrote Engels, "from the seventeenth century onwards, is England." At this time, the old feudal aristocracy and monarchy were being challenged by the newly emerged middle classes. The bastion of feudalism was the Roman Catholic church, which provided the divine justification for the monarchy and feudal institutions. This, therefore, had to be undermined before feudalism could be overthrown. The rising bourgeoisie challenged the old ideas and divine concepts that the old order was based upon.

"Parallel with the rise of the middle classes went on the great revival of science; astronomy, mechanics, physics, anatomy, physiology, were again cultivated. And the bourgeoisie for the development of its industrial production, required a science which ascertained the physical properties of natural objects and the modes of action of the forces of Nature. Now up to then science had but been the humble handmaid of the church, had not been allowed to overstep the limits set by faith, and for that reason had been no science at all. [In the 17th century, Galileo demonstrated the truth of Copernicus' theory that the earth and planets revolved around the sun. The professors of the day ridiculed these ideas and used the power of the Index and the Inquisition against Galileo to force him to recant his views - editor] Science rebelled against the church; the bourgeoisie could not do without science, and therefore, had to join in the rebellion." (Engels.)

It was at this time that Francis Bacon (1561-1626) developed his revolutionary ideas of materialism. According to him the senses were infallible and the source of all knowledge. All science was based upon experience, and consisted in subjecting the data to a rational method of investigation; induction, analysis, comparison, observation and experiment. It was, however, left to Thomas Hobbes (1588-1679) to continue and develop Bacon's materialism into a system. He realised that ideas and concepts were only a reflection of the material world, and that "it is impossible to separate thought from matter that thinks". Later, the English thinker John Locke (1632-1704) provided proof of this materialism.

The materialist school of philosophy passed from England to France, to be taken up and developed further by Rene Descartes (1596-1650) and his followers. These French materialists did not limit themselves to criticisms of religion, but extended them to all institutions and ideas. They challenged these things in the name of Reason, and gave ammunition to the developing bourgeoisie in their struggle with the monarchy. The birth of the great French Bourgeois Revolution of 1789-93 took as its creed materialist philosophy. Unlike the English Revolution in the mid-17th century, its French counter-part completely destroyed the old feudal order. As Engels later pointed out: "We know today that this kingdom of reason was nothing more than the idealised kingdom of the bourgeoisie."

The defect, however, of this materialism from Bacon onwards was its rigid, mechanical interpretation of Nature. Not accidentally, the English school of materialist philosophy flourished in the 18th century, when the discoveries of Isaac Newton made "mechanics" the most advanced and important science. In the words of Engels: "The specific limitation of this materialism lay in its inability to comprehend the universe as a process, as matter undergoing uninterrupted historical development."

The French Revolution had a profound effect upon the civilised world, similar to the Russian Revolution of 1917. It revolutionised thinking in every field, politics, philosophy, science and art. The ferment of ideas emerging from this bourgeois democratic revolution ushered in advances in natural science, geology, botany, chemistry as well as political economy.

It was in this period that a criticism was made of the mechanical approach of the materialists. A German philosopher, Immanuel Kant (1724-1804), made the first breakthrough in the old mechanistic ways with his discovery that the Earth and the solar system had come into being, and had not existed eternally. The same also applies to geography, geology, plants and animals.

This revolutionary idea of Kant was comprehensively developed by another brilliant German thinker, George Hegel (1770-1831). Hegel was a philosophical idealist, believing that the world could be explained as a manifestation or reflection of a "Universal Mind" or "Idea", i.e., some form of God.

Hegel looked upon the world not as an active participant in society and human history, but as a philosopher, contemplating events from afar. He set himself up as a measuring rod of the world, interpreting history according to his prejudices as the history of thought, the world as the world of ideas, an Ideal World. Thus for Hegel, problems and contradictions were posed not in real terms but in terms of thought, and could therefore find their solution only in terms of thought. Instead of contradictions in society being solved by the actions of men and women, by the class struggle, they instead find their solution in the philosopher's head, in the Absolute Idea!

Nevertheless, Hegel recognised the errors and shortcomings of the old mechanistic outlook. He also pointed out the inadequacies of formal logic and set about the creation of a new world outlook which could explain the contradictions of change and movement.

Although Hegel rediscovered and analysed the laws of motion and change, his idealism placed everything on its head. It was the struggle and criticism of the Young Hegelians, led by Ludwig Feuerbach (1804-1872), which tried to correct and place philosophy back on its feet. Yet even Feuerbach—"the under half of him was materialist, the upper half idealist" (Engels)—was not able to fully purge Hegelianism of its idealist outlook. This work was left to Marx and Engels, who were able to rescue the dialectical method from its mystical shell. Hegelian dialectics were fused with modern materialism to produce the revolutionary understanding of dialectical materialism.

What are Dialectics?

We have seen that modern materialism is the concept that matter is primary and the mind or ideas are the product of the brain. But what is dialectical thinking or dialectics?

"Dialectics is nothing more than the science of the general laws of motion and development of nature, human society and thought." (Engels, *Anti-Dühring*).

The dialectical method of thinking already had a long existence before Marx and Engels developed it scientifically as a means of understanding the evolution of human society.

The ancient Greeks produced some great dialectical thinkers, including Plato, Zeno and Aristotle. As early as 500 B.C., Heraclitus advanced the idea that "everything is and is not, for everything is in flux, is constantly changing, constantly coming into being and passing away". And further, "all things flow, all change. It is impossible to enter twice into one and the same stream". This statement already contains the fundamental conception of dialectics that everything in nature is in a constant state of change, and that this change unfolds through a series of contradictions.

"...the great basic thought that the world is not to be comprehended as a complex of ready made things, but as a complex of processes, in which things apparently stable, no less than their mental images in our heads, concepts go through an uninterrupted change of coming into being and passing away." (Engels, *Anti-Dühring*).

"For dialectical philosophy nothing is final, absolute, sacred. It reveals the transitory character of everything and in everything: nothing can endure before it except the uninterrupted process of becoming and of passing away, of endless ascendancy from the lower to the higher. And dialectical philosophy is nothing more than the mere reflection of this process in the thinking brain." (Ibid.)

Dialectics and Metaphysics

The Greek Philosophers brilliantly anticipated the later development of dialectics as of other sciences. But they could not themselves carry this anticipation to its logical conclusion owing to the low development of the means of production, and the lack of adequate information about the detailed workings of the universe. Their ideas gave a more-or-less correct general picture, but they were often more in the nature of inspired guesses than scientifically worked out theories. In order to carry human thought further, it was necessary to abandon these old methods to arrive at a general understanding of the universe, and concentrate on the smaller, more mundane tasks of collecting, sorting out and labelling a host of individual facts, of testing particular theories by experiment, of defining, etc.

This empirical, experimental, factual approach provided an enormous boost to human thought and science. Investigations into the workings of nature could now be carried out scientifically, analysing each particular problem and testing each conclusion. But in the process, the old ability to deal with things in their connection, not separately, in their movement, not statically, in their life not in their death, was lost. The narrow, empirical mode of thought which consequently arose is termed the "Metaphysical" approach. It still dominates modern capitalist philosophy and science. In politics it is reflected in Harold Wilson's famous "pragmatism" ("if it works, it must be right") and the constant appeals to "the Facts".

But facts do not select themselves. They have to be chosen by individuals. The order and sequence in which they are arranged, and the conclusions drawn from them depend upon the preconceived notions of the individual. Thus such appeals for "the Facts", which are supposed to convey the impression of scientific impartiality, are usually just a smokescreen to conceal the prejudices of the speaker.

Dialectics deals not only with facts, but with facts in their connection, i.e. processes, not only with isolated ideas, but with laws, not only with the particular, but with the general.

Dialectical thinking stands in the same relationship to metaphysics as a motion picture to a still photograph. The one does not contradict the other, but compliments it. However, the truer, more complete approximation of reality is contained in the movie.

For everyday purposes and simple calculations, metaphysical thought, or "common sense", suffices. But it has its limitations, and beyond these the application of "common sense" turns truth into its opposite. The fundamental shortcoming of this type of thinking is its inability to conceive of motion and development, and its rejection of all contradiction. However, movement and change imply contradiction.

"To the metaphysician things and their mental reflexes, ideas, are isolated, are to be considered one after the other and apart from each other, are objects of investigation, fixed, rigid, given once and for all. He thinks in absolutely irreconcilable antithesis. For him a thing either exists or does not exist: a thing cannot at the same time be itself and something else. Positive and negative absolutely exclude one another: cause and effect stand in rigid antithesis one to the other." (*Anti-Dühring*, p. 34.)

For everyday purposes, for instance, it is possible to say with a degree of certainty whether an individual, plant or animal is alive or dead. But in reality the question is not so simple, as legal cases on abortion and the "rights of the foetus" indicate. At what point precisely does human life begin? At what point does it end? Death, also is not a simple event but a protracted process, as Heraclitus understood: "It is the same thing in us that is living and dead, asleep and awake, young and old; each changes place and becomes the other. We step and we do not step into the same stream: we are and are not."

Trotsky, in his *ABC of Materialist Dialectics* characterised the dialectic as "a science of the forms of our thinking insofar as it is not limited to the daily problems of life but attempts to arrive at an understanding of more complicated and drawn-out processes."

He compared dialectics and formal logic (metaphysics) to higher and lower mathematics. It was Aristotle who first developed the laws of formal logic, and his system of logic has been accepted ever since by the metaphysicians as the only possible method of scientific thinking.

"The Aristotelian logic of the simple syllogism is accepted as an axiom for a multitude of practical human activities and elementary generalisations. The postulate starts from the proposition that 'A' = 'A'. But in reality 'A' is not equal to 'A'. This is quite easy to prove if we observe these two letters under a lens—they are quite different from each other. But, one can object, the question is not of the size or form of the letters, since they are only symbols for equal quantities, for instance, a pound of sugar. The objection is beside the point—in reality a pound of sugar is never equal to a pound of sugar—a more delicate scale will always disclose a difference. Again one can object; but a pound of sugar is equal to itself. Neither is this true—all bodies change uninterruptedly in size, weight, colour, etc. They are never equal to themselves. A sophist will respond that a pound of sugar is equal to itself 'at any given moment'. Aside from the extremely dubious practical value of the 'axiom' it does not withstand theoretical criticism, either. How should we really conceive the word 'moment' a purely mathematical abstraction, that is a zero of time? But everything exists in time: and existence itself is an uninterrupted process of transformation: time is subsequently a fundamental element of existence. Thus the axiom 'A' is equal to itself if it does not change, that is, if it does not exist.

"At first glance it could seem that these 'subtleties' are useless. In reality they are of decisive significance. The axiom 'A equals A' appears on the one hand to be the point of departure for all knowledge on the other hand the point of departure for all errors in our knowledge. To make use of the axiom 'A equals A' with impunity is possible only within certain limits. When quantitative changes in 'A' are negligible for the task at hand, then we can presume that 'A equals A'. This is, for example, the manner in which a buyer and a seller both consider a pound of sugar. We consider the Sun's temperature likewise. Until recently we considered the buying power of the dollar in the same way. But quantitative changes beyond certain limits become qualitative. A pound of sugar subjected to the action of water or Kerosene cease to be a pound of sugar. A dollar in the embraces of a president ceases to be a dollar. To determine the right moment, the critical point where quantity changes to quality is one of the most important and difficult tasks in all spheres of knowledge, including sociology." (Trotsky, *ABC of Materialist Dialectics*).

Hegel

The old dialectical method of reasoning, which had fallen into disuse from medieval times on, was revived in the early 19th century by the great German philosopher G.W.F. Hegel, (1770-1831). Hegel, one of the most encyclopaedic minds of his time, subjected the forms of formal logic to a detailed criticism, and demonstrated their limitations and one-sidedness. Hegel produced the first really comprehensive analysis of the laws of dialectics, which served as a basis upon which Marx and Engels later developed their theory of dialectical materialism. Lenin characterised Hegelian dialectics as "the most comprehensive, the most right in content and the most profound doctrine of development". In comparison with this, every other formulation was "one-sided and poor in content, and distorting and mutilating the real course of development (which often proceeds in leaps, catastrophes and revolutions) in nature and society". (Lenin, *Karl Marx*.)

Hegel's View of things was that of "A development that seemingly repeats the stages already passed, but repeats them differently, on a higher basis (negation of the negation), a development, so to speak, in spirals, not in a straight line; a development by leaps, catastrophes, revolutions; breaks in continuity; the transformations of quantity into quality; the inner impulses of development, imparted by the contradictions and conflict of the various forces and tendencies acting on a given body, or within a given phenomenon, or within a given society: the interdependence and the closest, indissoluble connection of all sides of every phenomenon (while history constantly discloses ever new sides), a connection that provides a uniform, a law-governed, universal process of motion, such are some of the features of dialectics as a richer (than the ordinary) doctrine of development?" (Ibid.)

"This new German philosophy culminated in the Hegelian system. In this system—and herein is its great merit—for the first time the whole world, natural, historical, intellectual, is represented as a process, i.e., as in constant motion, change, transformation, development; and the attempt made to trace out the internal connection that makes a continuous whole of all this movement and development. From this point of view the history of mankind no longer appeared as a wild whirl of senseless deeds of violence, as equally condemnable at the judgement-seat of mature philosophic reason, and which are best forgotten as quickly as possible, but as the process of evolution of man himself. It was now the task of the intellect to follow the gradual march of this process through all its devious ways and to trace out the inner laws running through all its apparently accidental phenomena." (Engels, *Anti-Dühring*, p.37.)

Hegel brilliantly posed the problem, but was prevented from solving it by his idealist preconceptions. It was, in Engels' words "a colossal miscarriage". Despite its mystical side, Hegel's philosophy already explained the most important laws of dialectics: Quantity and quality, the interpenetration of opposites and negation of the negation.

Quantity and Quality

"In spite of all gradualness, the transition from one form of motion to another always remains a leap, a decisive change". (Engels, *Anti-Dühring*.)

The idea of change and evolution is now generally accepted, but the forms by which changes occur in nature and society have only been explained by Marxian dialectics. The common view of evolution as a peaceful, smooth and uninterrupted development is both one-sided and false. In politics it is the "gradualist" theory of social change—the basic theoretical plank of reformism.

Hegel developed the idea of a "nodal line of measure relations"—in which at a definite nodal point, the purely quantitative increase or decrease gives rise to a qualitative leap: for example in the case of heated water, where boiling point and freezing point are the nodes at which under normal pressure the leap into a new state of aggregation takes place, and where consequently quantity is transformed into quality." (Engels, *Anti-Dühring*.)

Thus, in the example cited, the transformation of water from a liquid to vapour or solid ice do not occur by a gradual congealing or dissipation, but suddenly at a particular temperature (0°C, 100°C). The cumulative effect of numerous changes of the speed of the molecules eventually produces a change of state—quantity into quality.

Examples may be produced at will, from all the branches of science, from sociology and even from everyday life (e.g., the point at which the addition of salt changes the soup from something palatable to something undrinkable).

The Hegelian nodal line of measurement and the law of the transition of quantity into quality and vice-versa are of crucial importance not only to science (where, like other dialectical laws, they are used unconsciously by scientists who are not conscious dialecticians) but above all in an analysis of history, society and the movement of the working class.

The Interpenetration of Opposites

Just as "common sense" metaphysics seeks to eliminate contradiction from thought and revolution from evolution, it also tries to prove that all opposing ideas and forces are mutually exclusive. However, "we find upon closer examination that the two poles of an antithesis, positive and negative, e.g., are as inseparable as they are opposed, and that despite all their opposition they mutually interpenetrate. And we find, in like manner that cause and effect are conception to individual cases, but as soon as we consider the individual cases in their general connection with the universe as a whole, they run into each other, and they become confounded when we contemplate that universal action and interaction in which causes and effects are eternally changing places, so that what is effect here and now will be cause there and then and vice-versa". (Engels, *Anti-Dühring*, p.36.)

Dialectics is the science of inter-connections, in contrast to metaphysics which treats phenomena as separate and isolated. Dialectics seeks to uncover the countless threads, transition, cause and effect which bind together the universe. The first task of a dialectical analysis is therefore to trace the "Necessary connection, the objective connection of all the aspects, forces, tendencies etc., of the given sphere of phenomena". (Lenin, *Philosophical Notebooks*, p.97.)

Dialectics approaches a given phenomenon from the point of view of its *development*, its own movement and life; how it arises and how it passes away; it also considers the internal contradictory tendencies and sides of this thing.

Motion is the mode of existence of the entire material universe. Energy and matter are inseparable. Furthermore, motion is not imparted "from without", but the manifestation of the internal tensions that are inseparable not only from life, but from all forms of matter. Development and change takes place through internal contradictions. Thus dialectical analysis begins by laying bare by empirical investigation the inner contradictions which give rise to development and change.

From the dialectical standpoint all "polar opposites" are one-sided and inadequate, including the contradiction between "truth and error". Marxism does not accept the existence of any "Eternal Truths". All "truths" and "errors" are relative. What is true in one time and context becomes false in another: truth and error pass into each other.

Thus the progress of knowledge and science does not proceed from the mere negation of "incorrect theories". All theories are relative, grasping one side of reality. Initially they are assumed to have universal validity and application. They are "true". But at a certain point, deficiencies in the theory are noticed; they are not applicable to all circumstances, exceptions to the rule are found. These have to be explained, and at a certain point, new theories are developed which can account for the exceptions. But the new theories not only "negate" the old, but incorporate them in a new form.

We can exclude contradictions only by regarding objects as lifeless, at rest and individually juxtaposed, i.e. metaphysically. But as soon as we consider things in their motion and change, in their life, their mutual interdependence and interaction, we come up against a series of contradictions.

Motion itself is a contradiction between being in the same place and somewhere else at the same time.

Life, equally, is a contradiction that "a being is at each moment itself and yet something else". (Engels, *Anti-Dühring*, p.167.)

Living structures constantly absorb substances from the environment, assimilate them and simultaneously other parts of the body decay, disintegrate and are expelled. Constant transformations occur also in the world of organic nature; e.g., a rock which disintegrated under the pressure of the elements. Everything is therefore constantly itself and something else at one and the same time. Thus, the desire to eliminate contradictions is the desire to eliminate reality.

Negation of the Negation

Engels characterises this as "an extremely general and for this reason extremely far-reaching and important law of development of nature, history and thought; a law which ? holds good in the animal and plant kingdoms, in geology, in mathematics, in history and philosophy". (Ibid., p.193.)

This law, the workings of which were observed in nature long before it was written down, was first clearly elaborated by Hegel, who gives a whole series of concrete examples which are reiterated in *Anti-Dühring*. (Ibid., pp.186-190.)

The law of the negation of the negation deals with the nature of development through a series of contradictions, which appear to annul, or negate a previous fact, theory, or form of existence, only to be later negated in its turn. Motion, change and development thus moves through an uninterrupted series of negations.

However, negation in the dialectical sense does not signify a mere annulment or obliteration whereby the earlier stage is both overcome and preserved at the same time. Negation, in this sense, is both a positive and a negative act.

Hegel gives a simple example in his book, *The Phenomenology of the Mind*: "The bud disappears when the blossom breaks through, and we might say that the former is refuted by the latter; in the same way when the fruit comes the blossom may be explained to be a false form of the plant's existence, for the fruit appears as its true nature in place of the blossom. These stages are not merely differentiated, they supplement one another as being incomparable with one another. But the ceaseless activity of their own inherent nature makes them at the same time moments of an organic unity, where they do not merely contradict one another, but where one is as necessary as the other; and this equal necessity of all moments constitutes alone and thereby the life of the whole."

In this process of endless self-annulment, the disappearance of certain forms and the emergence of others, a pattern frequently emerges which seem to be a repetition of forms, events and theories already surpassed. Thus, it is a commonplace that "history repeats itself". Reactionary bourgeois historians have thus tried to prove that history itself is merely a meaningless repetition, proceeding in a never-ending circle.

Dialectics, on the contrary, discerns within these seeming repetitions an actual development from lower to higher, an evolution in which the same forms may repeat themselves, but on a higher level, enriched by previous developments.

This can be seen most clearly from the process of development of human ideas. Hegel already showed how philosophy developed through a series of contradictions; one school of thought negating another, but simultaneously absorbing the older theories into its own system of thought.

Similarly with the development of science. The alchemists of the Middle Ages were motivated for the search for the "Philosophers' Stone" which could turn base metal into gold. Owing to the low level of the productive forces and the lack of scientific technique, these early attempts at the "transmutation" of the elements was in reality a utopian fantasy. However, in the process of these vain attempts, the alchemists actually discovered a whole series of valuable facts about chemicals and experimental apparatus which later provided the basis of modern chemistry.

With the rise of capitalism, industry and technique, chemistry becomes a science which rejected the early "crazy" notions of the transmutation of the elements which was thus negated. However, all that was valuable and scientific in the discoveries of alchemy were preserved in the new chemistry, which maintained that the elements were "immutable" and could not be transformed one into another.

The 20th century has seen the revolutionising of science and technique with the discovery of nuclear physics, by means of which one element can actually be transformed into another. In fact, it would be theoretically possible to turn lead into gold, in modern times, but the process would be too expensive to be justified economically. Thus this particular process seems to have turned full circle:

(a) transmutation of elements (b) non transmutation of elements (c) transmutation of elements

But the repetition is only apparent. In reality, modern science, which in one sense has returned to an idea of the ancient alchemists, includes within itself all the enormous discoveries of the 19th century and 18th century science. Thus, one generation stands on the shoulders of another. Ideas which have apparently been "disproved" or "negated" make their re-appearance, but on a higher level, enriched by the previous experiences and discoveries.

Dialectics bases itself upon determinism: the thought that nothing in nature, society or thought is accidental; that seeming "accidents" arise only as the result of a deeper necessity.

Superficial historians have written that the First World War was "caused" by the assassination of a Crown Prince at Sarajevo. To a Marxist this event was an historical accident, in the sense that this chance event served as the pretext, or catalyst, for the world conflict which had already been made inevitable by the economic, political and military contradictions of imperialism. If the assassin had missed, or if the Crown Prince had never been born, the war would still have taken place, on some other diplomatic pretext. Necessity would have expressed itself through a different "accident".

Everything which exists, exists of necessity. But, equally, everything which exists is doomed to perish, to be transformed into something else. Thus what is "necessary" in one time and place becomes "unnecessary" in another. Everything begets its opposite which is destined to overcome and negate it. This is true of individual living things as much as societies.

Every type of human society exists because it is necessary at the given time when it arises: "No special order ever disappears before all the productive forces for which there is room in it, have been developed: and new higher relations of production never appear before the material conditions of their existence have matured in the womb of the old society. Therefore mankind always takes up only such problems as it can solve, since, looking at the matter more closely, we will always find that the problem itself arises only when the material conditions necessary for its solution already exist or at least are in the process of formation". (Marx, *Critique of Political Economy*.)

Slavery, in its day, represented an enormous leap forward over barbarism. It was a necessary stage in the development of productive forces, culture and human society. As Hegel put it: "It is not so much *from* slavery as *through* slavery that man becomes free".

Similarly capitalism was originally a necessary and progressive stage in human society. However, like slavery, primitive communism and feudalism (see section 2), capitalism has long since ceased to represent a necessary and progressive social system. It has foundered upon the deep contradictions inherent in it, and is doomed to be overcome by the rising forces of socialism, represented by the modem proletariat. Private ownership of the means of production and the nation state, the basic features of capitalist society, which originally marked a great step forward, now serve only to fetter and undermine the productive forces and threaten all the gains made in centuries of human development.

Capitalism is now a thoroughly decrepit, degenerate social system, which must be overthrown and replaced by its opposite, Socialism, if human culture is to survive. Marxism is determinist, but not fatalist, because the working out of contradictions in society can only be achieved by men and women consciously striving for the transformation of society. This struggle of the classes is not pre-determined. Who succeeds depends on many factors, and a rising, progressive class has many advantages over the old, decrepit force of reaction. But ultimately, the result must depend upon which side has the stronger will, the greater organisation and the most skilful and resolute leadership.

The Marxist philosophy is therefore essentially a guide to action: "Philosophers have only interpreted the world in various ways; the point is, however, to change it". (Marx, *Theses on Feuerbach*.)

The victory of socialism will mark a new and qualitatively different stage of human history. To be more accurate it will mark the end of the prehistory of the human race, and start a real history.

However on the other hand, socialism marks a return to the earliest form of human society—tribal communism—but on a much higher level, which stands upon all the enormous gains of thousands of years of class society. The economy of superabundance, will be made possible by the application of socialist planning to the industry, science and technique established by capitalism, on a world scale. This in turn will once and for all make redundant the division of labour, the difference between mental and manual labour, between town and countryside, and the wasteful and barbaric class struggle and enable the human race at least to set its resources to the conquest of nature: to use Engels' famous phrase, "Mankind's leap from the realms of necessity to the Realm of Freedom".

HISTORICAL MATERIALISM

When one looks at history, it appears to be a mass of contradictions. Events are lost in a maze of revolutions, wars, periods of progress and of decline. Conflicts of classes and nations swirl around in the chaos of social development. How is it possible to understand and explain these events, when it appears that they have no rational basis?

From the beginning, human beings have sought to discover the laws which govern their existence. Theories ranging from supernatural guidance to the leadership of "Great Men" have attempted in one way or another, at one time or another to provide such an explanation. Some believe that as people act independently of each other, theories of human development are utterly worthless.

For almost 2,000 years the ideas of *Genesis* dominated the outlook of Western Europe. Those who attempted to undermine this concept were branded as disciples of the Devil. It is only in very recent times that the "heretical" view of history, evolution, has been generally accepted although even then in a one-sided fashion.

For the capitalist class and their functionaries in the universities, schools and places of learning, history has to be taught in an academic and biased fashion with absolutely no relevance to the present day. They continue to peddle the myth that classes and private property have always existed in a bid to justify the "eternal" nature of capitalist exploitation and the economic anarchy inherent within it. Volumes and volumes have been written by leading academics and professors to disprove the writings of Marxism and above all its Materialist Conception of History.

Marxists attach enormous importance to the study of history; not for its own sake but so as to study the great lessons it contains. Without that understanding of the development of events, it is not possible to foresee future perspectives. Lenin, for example, prepared the Bolshevik Party for the October 1917 Revolution by a meticulous analysis of the experience of the Paris Commune and the events in Russia of 1905 and February 1917.

It is precisely in this sense that we study and learn from history. Marxism is the science of perspectives, using its method of Dialectical Materialism to unravel the complex processes of historical development.

Marxist philosophy examines things not as static entities but in their development, movement and life. Historical events are seen as processes. Evolution, however, is not simply the movement from the lower to the higher. Life and society develop in a contradictory way, through "spirals not in a straight line; a development by leaps, catastrophes, and revolutions; breaks in continuity; the transformation of quantity into quality; inner impulses towards development, imparted by the contradiction and conflict of the various forces and tendencies?" (Lenin.)

Engels expressed dialectics as being "the great basic thought that the world is not to be comprehended as a complex of ready-made things, but as a complex of processes, in which the things apparently stable no less than their mind images in our heads, the concepts, go through an uninterrupted change of coming into being and passing away?" (*Anti-Duhring*).

This method is also materialist in outlook. Ideas, theories, party programmes, etc., do not fall from the sky but always reflect the material world and material interests. As Marx explained, "the mode of production of material life conditioned the social, political and intellectual life processes in general. It is not the consciousness of men that determines their being, but on the contrary their social being that determines their consciousness".

Using this method, Marx was able to indicate "the way to an all embracing and comprehensive study of the processes of the rise, development, and decline of social-economic systems. People make their own history, but what determines the motives of people, of the mass of people, i.e. what gives rise to the clash of conflicting ideas and strivings? What is the sum total of all these clashes in the mass of human societies? What are the objective conditions of production of material life that form the basis of all of man's historical activity? What is the law of development of these conditions? To all these Marx drew attention and indicated the way to a scientific study of history as a single process which, with all its immense variety and contradictoriness, is governed by definite laws". (Lenin, *Three Sources and Component Parts of Marxism.*)

Primitive Communism

Early humans evolved some three million years ago out of a highly evolved species of ape. Slowly primitive "humans" moved away from the forests and into the plains; a transition which was accompanied by an improvement in the flexibility and dexterity of the hand. The posture of the body became more erect. Whereas other animals had different organs for defence (cutting digging, shovelling and coats for warmth), humans had none of these. To survive they had to develop their only resources which were their hands and brain. Through trial and error, humans learned various skills, which had to be handed down from one generation to another. Communication through speech became a vital necessity. As Engels explained, "mastery over nature began with the development of the hand, with labour, and widened man's horizon at every new advance". Men and women were social animals forced to band together and co-operate in order to survive. Unlike the rest of the animal kingdom, they developed the ability to generalise and think abstractly. Labour begins with the making of tools. With these tools, humans change their surrounding to meet their needs. "The animal merely uses its environment," says Engels, "and brings about changes in it simply by his presence; Man by his changes makes it serve his ends, masters it. This is the final, essential distinction between Man and other animals, and once again it is labour that brings about this distinction."

The economic forms were very simple. Humans, were very rare animals, and they roamed around in groups in search of food. This nomadic life was completely dominated with food gathering. Archaeologists call this period the old stone age. Henry Morgan, an early anthropologist, termed the period savagery. Then and for many thousands of years to come, private property did not exist. Everything that was made, collected, or produced was considered common property.

Between 10,000 and 12,000 years ago, a new higher period emerged known as the new stone age or Barbarism. Instead of roaming for food, advances were made in cultivating crops and domesticating animals. Men and women became free to settle in a particular place and as a result new tools were fashioned to assist the new work, and a food producing economy was created. Stable tribes and communities arose at this time. Even today, for a variety of reasons, many tribes in Africa, the South Pacific and South America exist at this stage of Barbarism.

Yet with the birth of the permanent settlement, private dwellings did not come into being; on the contrary, the large ones that were built were for common use. In this period, no private family existed. The children belonged to the entire tribe.

In the stage of primitive communism (savagery and barbarism, each being a lower and higher stage respectively), no private property, classes, privileged elites, police or special coercive apparatus (the state) existed. The tribes themselves were divided into social units called clans or gentes (singular gens). These, in fact, were very large family groups, which traced their descent from the female line alone. This is what is termed a matriarchal society. How else could it be when it was impossible to identify the real father of a child? It was forbidden for a man to cohabit with a woman from his own clan or gens, thus the tribes were made up from a coalition of clans. At certain times, a form of group marriage existed between the clans themselves.

This classless form of society was extremely democratic in its character. Everyone would participate in a general assembly to decide the important issues as they occurred, and their chiefs and officers would be elected for particular purposes. As Engels pointed out in his book, *The Origins of the Family, Private Property and the State*:

"How wonderful this gentle constitution is in all its natural simplicity! No soldiers, gendarmes and policemen, no nobility, kings, regents, prefects or judges, no prisons, no law-suits, and still affairs run smoothly. All quarrels and disputes are settled by the entire community involved in them, either the Gens or the tribe or the various Gentes amongst themselves. Only in very rare cases the blood revenge is threatened as an extreme measure. Our capital punishment is simply a civilised form of it, afflicted with all the advantages and drawbacks of civilisation. The communistic household is shared by a number of families, the land belongs to the tribe, only the gardens are temporarily assigned to the households. There cannot be any poor and destitute—the communistic households and the Gentes know their duties towards the aged, sick and disabled. All are free and equal—the women included. There is no room yet for slaves, nor for the subjection of foreign tribes".

To the narrow philistine, who sees private property as a sacred god, these societies are looked upon with contempt. To the tribespeople, private property is completely alien. "The Indians," explains the historian Heckewelder, "think that the great spirit has made the earth, and all that it contains, for the common good of mankind, when he stocked the country and gave them plenty of game, it was not for the good of the few, but of all. Everything is given in common to the sons of men. Whatever liveth on the land, whatever groweth out of the earth, and all that is in the rivers and waters was given jointly to all, and everyone is entitled to his share".

Common tribal property came under growing strain from the development with the private family, with private houses growing up alongside the communal dwellings. As time went on Common Land became later divided up to form the collective property of each family. The Matriarchal family gave way to the Patriarchal (male dominated) form, which became essential to the maintenance of the collective property.

This "family", however, must not be looked up on as similar to that of today. As Paul Lafargue says, "the family was not reduced to its last and simplest expression, as it is in our day, where it is composed of three indispensable elements: the father, the mother and the offspring; it consisted of the father, the recognised head of the family; of the legitimate wife, and his concubines, living under the same roof; of his children, his younger brothers, with their wives and children, and his unmarried sisters: such a family comprised many members".

The growth of private property in the later stages of primitive communism is regarded by Marxists as elements of the new society within the old. Eventually the qualitative accumulation of these new elements led to the qualitative break up of the old society.

With the growth of new means of production, particularly in agriculture, the question arose who should own them? The possession of tools, weapons, new metals, but above all the *means to make them*, enabled a family to rise above the terrible life and death struggle with the force of nature.

Then with the further development (trade developed at first between the different communities) of the productive forces, inequality began to appear within society. This had a profound effect upon the Old Order. For the first time, men and women were able to produce a *surplus* above and beyond his own needs, resulting in a revolutionary leap forward for humanity.

In the past, where war broke out between two tribes, it was uneconomic to take captives as slaves. After all, a captive would only have been able to produce sufficient food for himself. No surplus was produced. The only use for a captive, given the shortage of food, was as a source of meat. This was the economic foundation of cannibalism.

But once a surplus was produced, it became economically viable to keep a slave who was forced to work for his master. The surplus obtained from a growing number of slaves was then appropriated by the new class of slave owners. But how were the slaves to be controlled and forced to work? The old tribes had no police force or means of coercion. Every individual was free and was a warrior.

The production of a surplus product smashed the old forms of society, enabling classes to crystallise. The existence of these classes required an apparatus of force to subject one class by another. Rich and poor, landowner and tenant, creditor and debtor all made their appearance in society. The clans which were social units of originally blood relations, began to disintegrate. The rich of different clans had more in common with each other than they had with the poor of their own clan.

Slave Society

Despite all the horrors which accompanied it, the emergence of class society was enormously progressive in further developing society. For the first time since humans evolved from the ape, a section of society was freed from the labour of eking out an existence. Those who were freed from work could now devote their time to science, philosophy and culture. Class society brought with it priests, clerks, officials and specialised craftsmen. The historical justification and function of the new ruling class was to develop the productive forces and take society forward. It was at this stage that civilisation first emerged.

Special institutions were now created to protect the interests of the ruling class. Special armed bodies of men, with their gaols, courts, executioners, etc., as well as new laws were all needed to protect private property of the slave owner. The state together with its appendages came into being and the freedom and equality of the old gentile system fell into ruins. New ideas and morals developed to justify the new social and economic order.

By the 7th century B.C. the tribal aristocracy of Greece had become a ruling class of well-endowed slave owning landlords. According to the Ancient Greek philosopher, Aristotle, the majority of the population of Attica had been enslaved by this time.

With the growth of the city-states, the increase in the division of labour greatly accelerated. Not only between town and country, but between branches of trade and finance, merchant and usurer; new crafts sprung up together with a growing band of artists catering for the tastes and culture of the upper class.

The drive of the city-states for more and more slaves, resulted in continuous war. In the war against Macedonia by the Romans in 169 B.C., 70 cities in Epirus alone were sacked and 150,000 of their inhabitants sold as slaves. The slave economy was extremely wasteful and needed for its survival a continuous supply of slaves to replace those who had been injured or died. However the natural reproduction amongst slaves was very slow owing to the harshness of their lot, thus the only real method of replenishment was by conquest.

Although the slave was much less productive than the free peasant on the land, the low cost of his maintenance made slavery far more profitable. The ruination of the free peasants led to large numbers fleeing to the town forming the de-classed lumpenproletariat of the slave societies.

The latter relied upon the charity of the upper classes, who provided them with circuses for their amusement.

It was in this period that the revolutionary Christian movement emerged. Originally a group of primitive Communist sects with a deep hatred of the conquering Romans and their rich lackeys, they won much support from the poor and oppressed. These early Christian revolutionaries were prepared to use violent means to overthrow the upper classes and bring about "Heaven on Earth". They were therefore hounded by the authorities and were ruthlessly executed for treason against the Emperor. Later, Christianity was raised to the position of state religion after being purged of its class hatred. The ruling class used it as a weapon to dupe and pacify the lower classes into accepting their earthly lot and to encourage their illusions in a better life after death.

The greater the surpluses the slave-owners obtained from the exploitation of the slaves, the greater became their extravagance, brilliance, arrogance and idleness. As more and more wars had to be waged to increase the slave population by conquest, the Roman Empire overstretched itself. Wars cannot be fought without soldiers and the best soldiers were the peasants. They were rapidly disappearing and thus had to be replaced by highly paid foreign mercenaries. The age of the "cheap slave" came to a rapid end bringing with it the decline of the slave empires.

Despite the various slave rebellions—the most famous being led by Spartacus—the slave did not prove to be a revolutionary class that could take society forward. As Marx was to point out, the class struggle would end "either in a revolutionary reconstruction of society at large, or in the common ruin of the contending classes". Karl Kautsky, the German Marxist, explained that "the great migrations, the flooding of the Roman Empire by the swarms of savage Germans did not mean the premature destruction of a flourishing high culture, but merely the conclusion of a dying civilisation and the formation of the basis for a new upswing of civilisation".

The mighty slave civilisations had produced an enormous leap forward for society. One is amazed at the cultural achievements of Ancient Egypt and Babylon. The Greeks and Romans developed scientific knowledge to tremendous heights. Hero, the philosopher, had discovered the basic principles of the steam engine. The contributions of Archimedes, Pythagoras and Euclid advanced mathematics to the stage where the beginnings of mechanical engineering would have been possible. Nevertheless, slave society had reached its limits and internal decay and external factors were to bring it to destruction.

The Rise of Feudalism

"The last centuries of the declining Roman Empire and its conquest by the Barbarians destroyed a number of productive forces: agriculture had declined, industry had decayed for want of a market, trade had died out or had been violently suspended, the rural population and urban population had decreased." (Karl Marx, *The German Ideology*.)

Over the centuries, the barbarian masses overran Europe; in the East, the Goths, Germans and Huns; in the North and West, the Scandinavian; in the South, the Arabs. In their conquest of territories they proceeded to ransack the towns, and settle down in the countryside, where they lived by means of primitive agriculture.

In these communities, they elected their village chiefs, however, as time passed by, chiefs were always chosen from the same family. The head of the privileged family, through succession, became the natural chief. The villages were at constant war with their neighbours, resulting in conquered lands being divided up with the greater share accruing to the chief. He thus became the most powerful and propertied man in the community. In times of strife, he would guarantee the protection of those under him while in turn they were duty bound to grant military service to him. These peasants were later able to forgo their military service for a tribute in some form or another.

The authority of these village lords was extended into the surrounding countryside. The lord "owed justice, aid, and protection to his vassals, and these, in their turn, owed fidelity and homage to their lord". (Lafargue, *The Evolution of Property*.) Wars and conquests served to crystallise these feudal relationships. The lords and barons together with their men-at-arms formed a new social hierarchy, sustained by the labour provided by their vassals. As Lafargue expressed it: "So soon as the authority of the feudal nobility was constituted, it became in its turn, a source of trouble to the country whose defence it had been charged with. The barons, in order to enlarge their territories and thereby extend their power, carried on continual warfare among themselves, only interrupted now and again by a short truce necessitated by the tillage of the fields ? The vanquished, when not killed outright or utterly despoiled, became the vassals of the conqueror, who seized upon a portion of their lands and vassals. The petty barons disappeared for the benefit of the great ones, who became potent feudatories, and established ducal courts at which the lords in vassalage were bound to attend".

As feudal relations matured, the majority of farm land in Europe became divided into areas known as manors, each manor possessing its own lord and officials whose task was to manage the estate. The arable land was divided into two parts, about a third of it belonged to the lord (called a Demesne), while the rest was divided amongst his vassals. Pastures, wood and meadows were used as Common Land—a survival in fact from the days of Primitive Communism. Agriculture was to make great strides forward with the introduction of the three field system. The vassals share of the land, however, was further divided up into separate strips scattered throughout the fields which meant a massive drain on productivity.

The social structure which developed under feudalism, gave rise to new classes and groups. The social framework resembled a pyramid structure, headed by the king, aristocracy, the great churchmen and bishops. Under them were the privileged barons, dukes, counts and knights. On the bottom rungs of the social order were the freeman, serfs (Bordars, Cotters, Villeins), and slaves.

Unlike today, where the main body of wealth is created in the factories the land produced nearly all of social requirement. So land became the most important possession of the feudal system. The more land one held, the more powerful one became. The ruling class ruled by their virtual monopoly of land to which the serfs were tied. Theoretically, the King owned all the land but in reality areas and domains were granted to dukes, who in turn granted tenancy to counts, who would have many vassals under him granted tenancy of much smaller parcels of land. All had to provide services to their superiors in guaranteeing men-at-arms, payment of rent, etc.

Unlike the slave who owned nothing, the serf was a tenant of the lord. Unlike the slave, the serf has a vested interest in his plot of land. He had more rights than the slave: he could not be sold (neither could his family), providing some security, although the degree of serfdom and obligations varied. In return for this land and "rights", the serf was forced to work for the lord of the manor for certain periods of the week, without pay. Other services were demanded of him (Boon Days) at harvest time, and whenever the lord needed assistance. The lords' needs came first. The serf could not leave the land, had to have the lords' permission if his children were to marry outside his demesne. Taxes were imposed on a serf's inheritance and female heirs to land had to get the permission of their overlord.

The new organisation of society based on landed property gave rise to a further development of the productive forces. This time the surplus value created by the serf's labour was appropriated by the aristocratic lay and ecclesiastical ruling class.

In the words of the historian Meilly: "It is an economic maxim that productiveness increases in proportion as the freer constitution of society insures the workers an absolutely larger and more secure portion of the product of their labour. In other words, freer social forms have the direct effect of stimulating production."

As the new classes crystallised, new forms of state apparatus also came into existence to preserve the feudal property forms. The new morality and ideology that arose from these forms cemented social relationships. The Church, which became more and more powerful, provided the spiritual foundations of the new order and with it the Popes became more powerful than King or Emperor, with churchlands extending to between a third and a half of the land in Christendom. The tithe that is collected amounted to a 10 per cent tax on all income, goods, etc.

In general the feudal state remained centrally weak until the rise of the absolute monarchies of the 16th century. As a result, continual baronial wars shook the outlying provinces where robber barons built up their power and prestige, threatening the position of the central monarch. The struggle of the central monarch to subdue the regions is a characteristic feature of the period. The eventual defeat of these provincial lords, with their constant strife and war, enabled trade to develop to a higher level.

Trade was at a low level. The land, in fact, produced practically everything. It was a "natural" economy geared towards self-sufficiency. However, with the launching of the crusades, the expeditions to the Holy Land, new needs arose, and the merchants who supplied these needs, began to establish huge fairs in France, Belgium, England, Germany and Italy. These periodic fairs played an essential part in the growth of European trade, and helped to establish a strong class of rich merchants. Money relations began to erode the straight jacket of feudal society.

Hand in hand with the development of trade, went the growth of the towns. The merchant class that arose in the town clashed with the traditional standards and restrictions of feudalism.

The Church, for instance, considered the practice of usury as a sin, using the threat of excommunication against those who promoted it.

In his very good book, *Man's Worldly Goods*, Leo Huberinan explains the nature of the conflict: "The whole atmosphere of feudalism was one of confinement, whereas the whole atmosphere of merchant activity in the town was one of freedom. Town land belonged to feudal lords, bishops, nobles, kings. These feudal lords at first looked upon their town land in no different light from that in which they looked on the other land. All these forms (feudal dues, taxes, services) were feudal, based on the ownership of the soil. And all these forms had changed as far the towns were concerned. Feudal regulations and feudal justice were fixed by custom and difficult to alter. But trade by its very nature is active, changing, and impatient of barriers. It could not fit into the rigid feudal frame."

Therefore old relationships had to be challenged and changed. The towns began to demand their freedom and independence, and gradually town charters were conceded, some by agreement, others by force.

Trade itself gave rise to new forms of wealth. No longer was land the sole source of power and privilege, as money acquired in trading assumed a much greater importance. In the towns was born the wealthy merchant oligarchy which controlled and regulated the small scale individual production, through the guild system. With the further division of labour, Craft Guilds were established comprising the guild master, apprentices and journeymen. As more and more wealth was created through production the guild masters (employers of labour) came into sharp conflict with their journeymen (workers). By the 15th century, actual journeymen's unions were formed to protect their interests.

The introduction of the money economy (which had only a very limited character in slave society) slowly undermined the basis of the feudal system. Its laws and customs were modified to correspond with the new development. As serfs ran away to the towns to make their fortunes, money values began to transcend the old relationships, Labour dues being replaced by rented property. The impact of the Black Death, in the mid-14th century, greatly accelerated the process. Historians have estimated between 30 and 50 per cent of the population of England, Germany, the Low Countries, and France were wiped out by the Great Plague. This in turn resulted in the chronic shortage of labour, which forced many landowners to introduce wage labour to overcome their difficulties.

The Rise of the Absolute Monarch

The nation-state as we know it today did not always exist. Peoples' allegiances at this time belonged not to the nation but to the lord, the town, the locality, or the guild. People considered themselves not French, English, etc., but people of a town or city. Every Christian was a member of the Roman Catholic Church, which in turn ruled over Christendom, and thus was the greatest power of all.

With the growth of wealth in the towns, a capitalist class began to arise which demanded conditions suitable for the unhindered development of trade and commerce. They wanted order and security. The struggle for independence of the towns from their feudal overlords, the continuous battles between local barons, the pillaging that followed, all gave rise to the need for a central authority, a nation state.

The conflict between the central monarch and the great barons (a struggle between two sections of the ruling class) ended with a victory for the king. He was supported by the merchants and middle class, who provided the money to raise the armies he required. The emergence of the nation state together with the centralised monarchy ushered in a great economic advance. For their support, the monarch granted certain monopolies and privileges to sections of the middle class and the next stage was set for the clash between the national monarch and the interests of the international church.

The late 15th century saw the beginning of the voyages of discovery. Men such as Columbus and Vasco Da Gama were financed by rich merchants to seek new areas of exploitation and "spread the Word of God". Joint stock companies were established to promote the financing of greater exploitation, for plunder and profit.

With the massive profits from the voyages, many merchants and financiers became the real centres of power and wealth. Nobles, aristocrats and monarchs became debtors to the rich merchants. One banking family, the Fuggors, were even able to decide who was to be made Emperor of the Holy Roman Empire!

The new economic developments were giving rise to a capitalist formation. The basis of the feudal economy had begun to disintegrate with the growth in power and wealth of the rising bourgeoisie. New values, ideas, philosophies, and morals evolved out of the new relationships. The old ruling class stubbornly resisted the changes.

As Marx explained: "At a certain stage of development, the material productive forces of society come into conflict with the existing relation of production or—this merely expresses the same thing in legal terms—with the property relations within the framework of which they have operated hitherto. From forms of development of the productive forces these relations turn into their fetters. Then begins an era of social revolution". Later on, Marx adds: "No social order is ever destroyed before all the productive forces for which it is sufficient have been developed, and new superior relations of production never replace older ones before the material conditions for their existence have matured within the framework of the old society."

The old society has been undermined during the previous period. Probably one of the greatest challenges to the old order was the attack on Catholicism. In this period, the Church was not just a religious institution but the chief bulwark of the social order. Apart from being a powerful landowner, it collected a tithe from everyone, had its courts and special privileges, controlled education and shaped the political and moral outlook of the people. As Charles I once said: "People are governed by the pulpit more than the sword in times of peace." The Church censored books, and used the threat of excommunication against dissenters. It is said that this was a very religious period but this is wildly exaggerated by historians. Rather than people actually living according to the precepts of the Bible, religion was rather used to justify the Old Order. Everything, including political thought, was expressed in religious terms. Those who wished to undermine the system, had to first challenge the monopoly of Catholicism.

In the early 16th century, the absolute monarchies came into conflict with the Catholic Church themselves. The Protestant Reformation ushered in by Luther, supplied the weapons in the struggle against Papal power. In England, Henry VIII broke with Catholicism and raided the wealth of the monasteries, which was dissipated in expensive European and Irish wars.

The Capitalist Revolution

The Puritanism of the Calvin variety suited the outlook and morality of the rising middle class in town and country with its emphasis on self-reliance and personal success. The middle class was now set to rise quickly after adapting to the inflation rampant between 1540-1640, in which prices rose by more than fourfold and came increasingly into conflict with the old ruling class.

In England, the struggle between the new bourgeoisie and the old order took the form of the civil war. The New Model Army of Oliver Cromwell led the middle class into the armed struggle against the King and Old Order. In 1649, the King was beheaded and a capitalist republic declared. Cromwell, resting for support on the army, established himself as the head of a Bonapartist military dictatorship. The elements of left-wing democracy and its proponents (the Levellers and Diggers), who threatened capitalist property rights, had to be mercilessly quashed. From then on the regime rested on a narrow social basis—the armed forces. The capitalist regime under these critical crises circumstances reduced itself in the Bonapartist fashion to the rule of one man.

The feudal structures were dismantled together with the House of Lords and Monarchy. The old ruling class had been defeated, and the lower classes kept in their place. The struggle of the Parliamentarians against the King has been seen by historians and even by some contemporaries as a struggle against tyranny and for religious liberty but as Marx commented: "Just as one does not judge an individual by what he thinks about himself, so one cannot judge such a period of transformation by its consciousness, but on the contrary, this consciousness must be explained from the contradiction of material life, from the conflict existing between the social forces of production and the relations of production".

Leon Trotsky, one of the leaders of the Russian Revolution, once noted: "Revolutions have always in history been followed by counter-revolutions. Counter-revolutions have always thrown society back, but never as far back as the starting point of the revolution". So it was in 1660 and 1689, where the big bourgeoisie hurriedly made a compromise with the "bourgeois" elements of the aristocracy. The monarchy and House of Lords were restored although from then on they could never play the same role as their predecessors, on the contrary, they became part and parcel of the capitalist state. The bourgeois men of property concerned themselves with their future, and of keeping the lower orders in their place with their power carefully checked.

One hundred years later, the French Capitalist revolution was carried through to completion without any compromise being struck. The French Revolution, like its English counter-part, began with a split in the ruling class. The King and his ministers clashed over a scheme to avoid state bankruptcy, with the Parliament (which represented the nobility, higher clergy, the court clique, etc.). The latter's appeal against the government tyranny took on unforeseen flesh and rioting broke out in the streets of the towns and cities. It brought to a head all the simmering discontent of the middle class and lower orders against the regime. "The revolt of the nobility was," explains George Rude, "perhaps, a curtain-raiser rather than a revolution which, by associating the middle and lower classes in common action against King and aristocracy, was unique in contemporary Europe." Despite the attempts at reform from above, they were insufficient to prevent revolution from below.

As in all popular revolutions the masses burst onto the scene of history. The most self-sacrificing came to the fore, and pushed the revolution far to the left. Between 1789 and 1793 the old feudal regime and aristocracy had been completely swept away. The regime was headed by the revolutionary middle class, the Jacobins, who were supported and pushed by the plebeian masses made up of wage-earners and small craftsmen. A shift to the right occurred in 1794 with the government of the Directory coming to power. This in its turn gave way to a new political counter-revolution, which brought to power the law and order type regime of Napoleon Bonaparte. Nevertheless, the old order had been broken, and the new bourgeois property rights were to remain intact. The shift of political power was not accompanied by a social change backwards, i.e., it did not bring a return to the feudal order but was a political change brought about through the struggles of different sections of the capitalist class itself.

The Triumph of Capitalism

The great Bourgeois revolutions cleared the path for capitalism. The agrarian changes ensured the growth of capitalist agriculture, where the old feudal estates had been broken up and distributed to the peasants. In England, the conversion of a section of the aristocracy before the revolution prepared the way for the ruination of the peasantry itself. Governments now, instead of acting as a brake on trade and industry, actually championed its cause.

Through robbery, enclosure and plunder and competition, the means of production became concentrated into fewer and fewer hands. The ruination of the peasantry provided a pool of labour-power in the towns and cities. The class structure became more simplified. On the one hand were the capitalists and on the other the propertyless proletarians. All that these workers possessed was their ability to work. The only way they could remain alive was to sell their labour-power to the capitalists in return for wages. In the process of production, the proletarian produces more value than he receives in wages, the surplus value being expropriated by the capitalists. In its search for profit, amidst competition from rivals, the capitalist class is forced to introduce new methods of production, in this way capitalism has, historically, played a progressive role continually revolutionising the productive forces.

Its export of commodities and then capital leads the capitalist class to create "a world after its own image". The productive forces, technique and science gradually outgrew the nation state which protected it.

Rise of Imperialism

The period from 1870 to 1900 saw the division of the world amongst the main powers. In 1870 one-tenth of Africa had been divided up; by 1900 some nine-tenths of the "Dark Continent" were in the hands of Britain, France or one of the other European Empires. By 1914 this process of world division had been completed, and capitalism entered its highest stage of Imperialism. Huge trusts and monopolies had grown out of the earlier period of competition. "The state had more and more fused with the monopolies and financial institutions and acted increasingly in their interest. Production in this epoch is accompanied by the export of capital itself." (Lenin)

The imperialist stage brings with it the threat of world war, in the struggle for new markets, etc. Due to the carving up of the world and the tremendous growth in production, markets can now only be obtained by a new re-division of the world which inevitably leads to conflict on a world scale. World war indicates the contradictions between the private ownership of the means of production on the one hand and the nation state on the other. But unlike previous societies Capitalism has furnished the material pre-requisites for the new socialist order that can guarantee plenty for all.

The proletariat is the only consistent revolutionary class capable of carrying through to a conclusion the socialist revolution. This stems from its particular place in social production. The working class is disciplined in the factories and forced to co-operate in the productive process. It organises itself into large trade unions and then into its own independent party. Marxism, as opposed to all other theories, provides it with a clear ideology and tasks in its mission to overthrow capitalism. The Bolshevik Party, led by Lenin and Trotsky, provided a living model to the workers of the world.

The peasantry and the middle classes are incapable of playing a leading role, due to their social position. The peasantry is scattered in the countryside, and have no real conception of unity or internationalism. These middle layers of society follow either the bourgeoisie or the proletariat.

The peasantry have been in fact, the classical tool of Bonapartism—a regime based on the armed forces, balancing between the classes. In the epoch of imperialism and the decay of monopoly capitalism, if the working class fails to win the middle layers to its Socialist banner, they will be driven into the arms of reaction.

The Law of Uneven and Combined Development

From a progressive social system, capitalism has now become a fetter upon production and the further development of humanity. Marx believed that the proletariat would come to power first in the advanced capitalist countries of Britain, Germany, and France. However, with the emergence of imperialism, capitalism, in the words of Lenin, "broke at its weakest link" in backward Russia.

Society does not develop in a straight line, but according to its laws of uneven and combined development. The uneven growth of society on the world scale is constantly cut across by the introduction of new products and ideas from different social systems. The backwardness of semi-feudal Russia was supplemented by the most modern techniques of production in its cities, due to the enormous amount of foreign capital from France and Britain. The new industrial proletariat which had recently come into being accepted the most advanced ideas of the working class: Marxism.

In many of the under-developed countries the festering sores of much needed land reform, autocracy, national oppression, and economic stagnation, have resulted in enormous discontent. The tasks of the bourgeois democratic revolution, which would have laid the basis for capitalist development, have either only been partially carried out or not at all.

In these countries the capitalist class has come on the scene too late to play a similar role as its revolutionary counter-part of the 17th and 18th century. As in Russia before 1917, they are too weak and tied by a thousand strings—through marriage and mortgage—to the land owners and imperialists. They both now acquire a common hatred of the emerging proletariat. The nationalist capitalist class prefers to cling to the old order rather than appeal to the lower classes to carry through the anti-feudal revolution.

The only class capable of carrying out the revolution is the proletariat by uniting around itself the poorer sections of the peasantry. Once the working class comes to power as in October 1917, it is then able to give the land to the peasants, expel the imperialists and unify the country. However, the proletariat would not stop at these measures but would then proceed to the socialist tasks: nationalisation of the basic industries, land, and financial institutions.

The Russian Revolution was the greatest event in the whole of human history. For the first time the working class took power, swept out the capitalists, landlords and gangsters and organised a "democratic workers' state". It was to be the beginning of the international socialist revolution and fully confirmed the theory of Permanent Revolution.

Unfortunately, the betrayal of the socialist revolution in Germany, and other countries, led to the isolation of the revolution in a backward, devastated country. The destruction of the War, mass illiteracy, civil war, exhaustion, placed terrible strains upon the weak working class, and contributed to the degeneration of the revolution. It was these objective conditions which encouraged the growth of bureaucratism in the state, trade unions and the Party. Stalin rose to power on the back of this new bureaucratic caste. The individual in history represents not himself, but the interests of a group, caste or class in society.

Stalinism and its monstrous dictatorship grew not from the Bolshevik Party or socialist revolution, but out of the isolation and material backwardness of Russia. It destroyed the workers' democracy in order to preserve its privileges and power.

The Stalinist regime nevertheless rested on the new property forms of nationalised industry and the plan of production. The Soviets (Workers' Councils) and workers' democracy were crushed in the Stalinist *political counter-revolution*. Only by a new *political* revolution could the Russian working class have restored the workers' democracy which existed under Lenin and Trotsky. This would not mean a return to capitalism, but an end to the privileged bureaucratic elite, as the masses themselves become involved in the running of society and the state.

The Socialist Revolution

The socialist transformation ushers in a new and higher form of society by breaking the fetters on the development of the productive forces. The obstacle of private property and the nation state are swept away, allowing the socialised property to be planned in the interests of the majority.

The socialist revolution cannot be confined to one country, but puts the world revolution on the order of the day. The world economy and the world division of labour created by capitalism demands an international solution. A Socialist United States of Europe would prepare the ground for a World Federation of Socialist States, and the international planning of production. This in turn would provide the basis for the "planned and harmonious production of goods for the satisfaction of human wants".

One of the first tasks of the victorious working class would be the destruction of the old state machine. In all class societies the state came into existence as "an organ of class rule, an organ for the oppression of one class by another". This raises the question, does the working class need a state? The anarchists reply no. But they fail to understand that some form of force is required to keep the old landowners, bankers and capitalists in their place. The proletariat therefore has to construct a new type of state to represent its interests. In a workers' state, the majority are holding a tiny minority of ex-capitalists in check and therefore the massive bureaucratic state of the past is not needed. This "Dictatorship of the Proletariat" or Workers' Democracy, as Trotsky preferred to call it, vastly broadened and extended the highest forms of bourgeois democracy.

Bourgeois democracy was defined by Marx as the workers deciding every five years which section of the ruling class would misrepresent their interests in Parliament. Everyone could say what they liked, provided that the boards of the monopolies could actually decide what was to be done.

The new workers state would extend democracy from the political to the economic sphere with the nationalisation of the major monopolies.

New organs of power, such as the Soviets in Russia, based on the armed people, constitute "working bodies, executive and legislative at the same time". Bureaucracy would be replaced by the involvement of the masses in the running of the state and society. In order to prevent the growth of officialdom, the proletariat of Paris in 1871 and of Russia in 1917 introduced the following measures:

(1) Election of all officials, with the right to recall. (2) No standing army, but an armed people. (3) No official to receive more than a skilled worker. (4) Positions in the state to be rotated amongst the people.

With the reduction of the working week, the masses are given the opportunity to involve themselves in the state, and obtain the key to culture, science and art. For as Engels once said, if art, science and government remain the preserve of the minority, they will use and abuse this position in their own interest, as was the case in the Stalinist countries.

The state arose historically with the emergence of class society. Thus, from its very inception, the workers' state begins to *wither away*, as classes themselves dissolve within society. This is why Engels characterised the proletarian state as a "semi-state".

"Under socialism much of 'primitive' democracy will inevitably be revived, since, for the first time in the history of civilised society, the *mass* of the people will rise to taking an *independent* part, not only in voting and elections, *but also in the everyday administration of the state*. Under Socialism all will govern in turn and will soon become accustomed to no one governing". (Lenin, *The State and Revolution*.)

In this lower stage of socialism as Marx called it, one sees society, "just as it *emerges* from capitalist society; which is thus in every respect, economically, morally and intellectually, still stamped with the birthmarks of the old society from whose womb it comes". (Marx, *Critique of the Gotha Programme*.) *Although the exploitation of man by man* has been ended, production has not yet reached a high enough level to completely eradicate inequality or class differences. People still have to follow the principle: "He who does not work shall not eat". The state, despite its transitory character, remains the guardian of inequality.

Socialism, the Classless Society

Yet with huge strides forward in production, based on the most advanced science and conscious planning, humanity enters the higher realms of real society. Classes and the state will have completely withered away, as society now adopts the slogan "From each according to his ability, to each according to his needs". The antitheses of town and country, and mental and physical labour disappear with the further revolution in the productive forces. In the words of Lenin, "the narrow horizon of bourgeois law", which compels one to calculate with the heartlessness of a Shylock whether one has not worked half an hour more than somebody else, whether one is getting less pay than somebody else—this narrow horizon will then be left behind. There will then be no need for society, in distributing the products, to regulate the quantity to be received by each; each will take freely according to his needs.

The barbarous nature of class society would have ended once and for all. The prehistory of humankind would have been completed. The productive forces built up over thousands of years of class rule now laid the basis for classless society where the state and division of labour were rendered superfluous. Humanity sets itself the task of conquering nature, and opens up the tremendous wonders of science and technology. In the words of Engels, "the government of persons is replaced by the administration of things".

And Trotsky pointed out that, "Once he has done with the anarchic forces of his own society man will set to work on himself, in the pestle and retort of the chemist. For the first time mankind will regard itself as raw material, or at best as a physical and psychic semi-finished product. Socialism will mean a leap from the realm of necessity into the realm of freedom in this sense also, that the man of today, with all his contradictions and lack of harmony, will open the road for a new and happier race". (Leon Trotsky, *In Defence of October.*)

MARXIST ECONOMICS

Today, under the impact of the capitalist crisis, many workers have developed a thirst for economics. They are attempting to understand the forces which dominate their lives. This brief introduction to Marxist economics attempts to provide the class conscious worker not with a complete account of economics, but a guide to the basic laws of motion of capitalist society dominating his existence.

The shallowness of capitalist economics is demonstrated by their inability to understand the crisis affecting their system. Its role is to cover up the exploitation of the working class and to "prove" the superiority of capitalist society. Their quack "theories" and "solutions" are incapable of patching up the rotten and diseased nature of capitalism. Only the transformation of society on socialist lines and the introduction of a planned economy can end the nightmare of unemployment, slump and chaos.

The right wing labour leaders have rejected their old god Keynes, to be replaced by "orthodox" economic solutions: cuts, wage restraint and deflation. The left reformists still cling to the capitalist policies of yesterday (reflation, import controls, etc.), which have been recognised as totally ineffective under capitalism.

Only with a Marxist understanding of capitalist society can the conscious worker cut through the lies and distortion of the capitalist economists and combat their influence within the labour movement.

Conditions of Capitalism

Today, modern production is concentrated in the hands of giant companies. Unilever, ICI, Fords, British Petroleum, are some examples of the firms which dominate our lives. Although it is true that small businesses do exist, they really represent the production of the past and not the present. Modern production is essentially a mass, large-scale business.

At present, 200 top companies together with 35 banks and finance houses control the British economy, and account for 85 per cent of output. This development has come about over the past few hundred years through ruthless competition, crisis and war. At the time when the classical economists predicted free trade in the future, Marx explained the development of monopoly from competition as the weaker firms went to the wall. Monopoly capitalism grew out of and abolished free competition.

At first sight, it looks as if goods and things are produced mainly for people's needs. Obviously every society has to do this. But under capitalism, goods are not merely produced to satisfy someone's want or need, but primarily for sale. That is the paramount function of capitalist industry.

In the famous words of the ex-chairman of British Leyland, Lord Stokes, "I'm in business to make money, not cars!" This is a perfect expression of the aspirations of the entire capitalist class.

The capitalist process of production requires the existence of certain conditions. Firstly, the existence of a large class of propertyless workers who are obliged to sell themselves piece-meal in order to live. Thus the Tory conception of a "property owning democracy" is an absurdity under capitalism, because if the mass of the population owned sufficient property to be self-sufficient, the capitalists would not find the workers to produce their profits. Secondly, the means of production must be concentrated in the hands of the capitalists. Over the centuries, the peasants and those who owned their own means of subsistence were ruthlessly crushed and their means of life appropriated by the capitalists and landlords. They in turn hire the workers to work these means of production and produce surplus value.

Value and Commodities

How does capitalism work? How are workers exploited? Where does profit come from? How are slumps caused?

In order to answer these questions, we first need to learn the key to the mystery: what is value? Having solved this problem, the other answers fall into place. An understanding of value is essential, for an understanding of the economics of capitalist society.

To begin with, all the capitalist firms produce goods or services, or more correctly they produce commodities. That is a good or service produced for sale only. Of course, someone may make something for his or her own personal use. Before capitalism existed, many people had to. But this is not a commodity. Capitalist production is above all the creation and "immense accumulation of commodities". That is why Marx himself started his investigation of capitalism with an analysis of the character of the commodity itself.

Every commodity has a use-value for people. That means they are useful to someone otherwise they could not be sold. This use-value is limited to the physical properties of the commodity.

They also contain a value. What is it and how can it be shown?

If we leave the use of money out for the time being, commodities, when they are exchanged, fall into certain proportions.

For example:

1 pair of shoes)
1 watch) = 10 yards of cloth
3 bottles of whisky)
1 car tyre)

Each of the items on the left can be exchanged for 10 yards of cloth. They also, in the same amounts, can be exchanged with one another.

This simple example shows that the exchange value of these different commodities expresses something contained in them. But what makes a pair of shoes = 10 yards of cloth? Or 1 watch = 3 bottles of whisky? And so on?

Well, obviously, there must be something common to all. Clearly it is neither weight, colour, nor hardness. Again, it is not because they are useful. Bread after all is worth less than a Roll Royce, yet one is a necessity and the other luxury. So what is the common quality? The only thing in common is they are all products of *human labour.*

The amount of human labour contained in a commodity is expressed in time: weeks, days, hours, minutes.

To go back to the example: all these commodities can be expressed in terms of their common factor, labour-time.

5 hours (labour) worth of shoes
5 hours (labour) worth of tyres
5 hours (labour) worth of watches
5 hours (labour) worth of whisky
5 hours (labour) worth of cloth

Average Labour

If we look at commodities as use-values (their utility), we see them as a "shoe", "watch", etc., as products of a particular kind of labour the labour of the cobbler, watchmaker, etc. But in exchange, commodities are looked at differently. The special character is lost sight of and they appear as so many units of average labour. In exchange we are now comparing the amounts of human labour in general contained in the commodities. All labour, in exchange, is reduced to average simple units of labour.

It is true that the commodity produced by skilled labour contains more value than that produced by unskilled. Therefore in exchange, the units of skilled labour are reduced to so many units of unskilled, simple labour. For example, the ratio of 1 skilled unit = 3 unskilled units, or simply skilled labour is worth three times as much as unskilled.

Explained simply, the value of commodity is determined by the amount of average labour used in its production (or how long it takes to produce). But left like this, it appears that the lazy worker produces more values than the most efficient worker!

Let us take the example of a shoemaker who decides to use the out-dated methods of the Middle Ages to produce shoes. Using this method, it takes him a whole day to make a pair of shoes. When he tries to sell them on the market, he will find that they will only fetch the same as shoes produced by the better equipped more modern factories.

If these factories produce a pair of shoes in, say half an hour, they will contain less labour (and therefore less value) and will be sold cheaper. This will drive the shoemaker using medieval methods out of business. His labour producing a pair of shoes after half an hour is wasted labour, and unnecessary under modern conditions. On pain of extinction he will be forced to introduce modern techniques and produce shoes at least equal to the necessary time developed by society.

At any given time, using the average labour, machines, methods, etc., all commodities take a particular time to make. This is governed by the level of technique in society. In the words of Marx, all commodities must be produced in a socially necessary time. Any more labour-time spent over and above this will be useless labour, causing costs to rise and making the firm uncompetitive.

So to be more precise, the value of a commodity is determined by the amount of socially necessary labour in the article. Naturally, this labour time is continually changing as new techniques and methods of work are introduced. Competition drives the inefficient to the wall.

Thus we can also understand why precious gems have more value than everyday items. More socially necessary labour time is needed to find, and extract the gems, than the production of ordinary commodities. Their value therefore being considerably higher.

Again a thing can be a use value without having any value, i.e. a useful thing that has had no labour time spent on its production: air, rivers, virgin soil, natural meadows, etc. Therefore labour is not the only source of wealth, i.e. use values, but nature too is a source.

From the above we can see that an increase in productivity will increase the amount of things produced (material wealth), but can reduce the value of the things concerned, i.e. the amount of labour in each commodity is less. Increased productivity therefore results in an increase in wealth. With two coats two people can be clothed, with one coat only one person. Nevertheless, the increase in the quantity of material wealth may correspond with a fall in the magnitude of its value.

Money

As a result of the difficulties in exchange by using the methods of barter, more frequently a common article was used as "money". Over the centuries one commodity—gold—became singled out to play this role as the "universal equivalent".

Instead of saying a good is worth so much butter, meat, cloth, etc., it became expressed in terms of gold. The money expression of value is price. Gold was used because of its qualities. It concentrates much value in a small amount, can easily be divided into coins, and is also hard wearing.

As with all commodities, the value of gold itself is determined by the amount of labour-time spent on its production. For example, say it takes 40 hours labour to produce one ounce of gold. Then all the other goods that take the same time to produce are equal to that ounce of gold. Those that take half the time equal half the amount, etc.

One ounce of gold = 40 hours labour
1/2 ounce of gold = 20 hours labour
1/4 ounce of gold = 10 hours of labour
Therefore:
One car (40 hours labour) = 1 ounce of gold
One table (10 hours labour) = 1/4 ounce of gold

Due to the changes in productive technique and the increase in the productivity of labour, all the values of commodities are continually fluctuating, like so many trains in a station pulling in and out at differing times. If you take any train as a standard which is moving off to gauge the movement of others, it would lead to confusion. Only by standing on the firm platform can you judge accurately what is happening. In relation to the changes of all goods, gold acts as the measure. Although the most stable, even this is in constant motion, as no commodity has a totally fixed value.

Prices of Commodities

The law of value governs the price of goods. As explained earlier, the value of commodities is equal to the amount of labour contained in it. In theory, the value is equal to its price. Yet, in reality, the price of a commodity tends to be either above or below its real value. This fluctuation is caused by different influences on market price, such as the growth of monopoly. The differences of supply and demand also have a great effect. For instance, there may be a surplus of a commodity in the market, and the price that day may be far below the real value, or if there was a shortage, the price would rise above it. The effects of supply and demand have led bourgeois economists to believe that this law is the sole factor in determining price. What they were unable to explain was that prices always fluctuate around a definite level. What that level is, is not determined by supply and demand, but by the labour time spent in the articles' production. A lorry will always be more expensive than a plastic bucket.

Profits

Some "clever" people have invented the theory that profits arise from buying cheap and selling dear. In *Wage, Labour and Capital,* Marx explains the nonsense of this argument:

"What a man would certainly win as a seller he would lose as a purchaser. It would not do to say that there are men who are buyers without being sellers or consumers without being producers. What these people pay to the producers, they must first get from them for nothing. If a man first takes your money and afterwards returns that money in buying your commodities you will never enrich yourself by selling your commodities too dear to that same man. This sort of transaction might diminish a loss, but would help in realising a profit".

Labour Power

In obtaining the "factors of production", the capitalist looks on the "labour market" as just another branch of the general market for commodities. The abilities and energies of the worker are seen as just another commodity. He advertises for so many "hands".

What we have to be clear about is what the capitalist has bought. The worker has sold not his labour but his ability to work. This Marx calls his *labour power*.

Labour power is a commodity governed by the same laws as other commodities. Its value is determined by the labour-time necessary for its production. Labour power is the ability of the worker to work. It is "consumed" by the capitalist in the actual labour-process. But this presupposes the existence and health and strength of the worker. The production of labour power therefore means the worker's self-maintenance and the reproduction of his species, to provide new generations of "hands" for the capitalist.

The labour-time necessary for the worker's maintenance is the labour-time it takes to produce the means of subsistence for him and his family: food, clothing, fuel, etc. The amount of this varies in different countries, different climates, and different historical periods. What is adequate subsistence for a labourer in Calcutta would not be adequate for a Welsh miner. What was adequate for a Welsh miner fifty years ago would not be for a Midlands car worker today. Into this question, unlike the value of other commodities, there enters a historical and even moral element. Nevertheless, in any given country, at any particular stage of historical development, the "standard of living" is known. (Incidentally, it is precisely the creation of new needs which is the spur to all kinds of human progress).

Not Cheated!

Apart from the daily reproduction of his labour power, and the reproduction of the species, at a certain stage in the development of capitalist technique, a certain amount has to be provided for the education of the workers in order to fit them for the conditions of modern industry and raise their productivity.

Unlike most commodities, labour power is paid for only after it has been consumed. The workers thus philanthropically extend credit to their employers! (weeks in hand, petty cheating and bankruptcy, leading to loss of wages).

Despite this, the worker has not been cheated. He has arrived at an agreement of his own free will. As with all other commodities, equivalent values are exchanged: the worker's commodity, labour power, is sold to the boss at the "going rate". Everybody is satisfied. And if the worker is not, then he is free to leave and find work elsewhere - if he can?

The sale of labour power poses a problem. If "nobody is cheated", if the worker receives the full value of his commodity, where does exploitation come from? Where does the capitalist make his profits? The answer is that the worker sells the capitalist not his labour (which is realised in the work process), but his labour power—his ability to work.

Having purchased this as a commodity, the capitalist is free to use it as he pleases. As Marx explained: "From the instant he steps into the work shop, the use-value of his labour power, and therefore also its use, which is labour, belongs to the capitalist".

Surplus Value

We will see from the following example that the capitalist purchases labour power because it is the only commodity which can produce new values above and beyond its own value.

Let us take a worker who is employed to spin cotton into yarn. He gets paid £1 per hour and works an 8 hour day.

After 4 hours he had produced 100lbs of yarn at a total vale of £20. This value of £20 is made up from the following:

Raw materials £11 (cotton, spindle, power)

Depreciation £1 (wear and tear)

New value £8

The new value created is sufficient to pay the workers' wages for the full 8 hours. At this point the capitalist has covered all his costs (including his total wage bill). But as yet no surplus value (profit) has been produced.

During the next 4 hours another 100lbs of yarn is produced valued again at £20. And again £8 of new value is created, but this time the wages have already been covered. Therefore this new value (£8) is surplus value. From this comes rent (to the landlord), interest (to the moneylender) and profit (to the industrialist). Thus surplus value or profit, in the words of Marx, is the unpaid labour of the working class.

The Working Day

The secret of the production of surplus value is that the worker continues to work longer after he has produced the value necessary to reproduce the value of his labour power (his wages). "The fact that half a day's labour is necessary to keep the labourer alive does not in any way prevent him from working a full day." (Marx).

The worker has sold his commodity and cannot complain about the way he is used, any more than the tailor can sell a suit and then demand that his customer must not wear it as often as he likes. The working day is therefore so organised as to give the maximum benefits from the labour power he has bought. In this lay the secret of the transformation of money into capital.

Constant Capital

In production itself, machines and raw materials lose their use value, they become burnt up and become absorbed into the new product. They transfer their value into the new commodity.

This is clear in relation to raw materials (wood, metal, dyes, fuel, etc.) which are wholly consumed in the process of production, only to reappear in the properties of the article produced.

Machines on the other hand, do not disappear in the same way. But they do deteriorate in the course of production, thus dying a protracted death. The exact moment when a machine is finally declared redundant is no more possible to fix with exactitude than the exact moment of a person's death. But just as the insurance company, on the basis of the theory of averages, makes very accurate (and profitable) calculations concerning the life-span of men and women, so the capitalist know by experience and calculation roughly how long a machine will last.

The depreciation of machinery, its daily loss of use value, is calculated on this basis and added on to the cost of the article produced. Thus, the means of production add to the commodity their own value in proportion as the deterioration of its use value unfolds. The means of production, therefore, cannot transfer to the commodity more than that value which they themselves lose in the process of production. It is thus called constant capital.

Variable Capital

While the means of production add no new value to the commodities produced, but only deteriorate, the labour of the worker not only preserves, but adds new value to his product by merely working. If the process of work were to stop at that moment when the worker had produced articles to the value of his own labour power, e.g. in 4 hours (£8) this is the only bit of new value created.

But the work process does not stop there. This would only cover the expenses of the capitalist in hiring the workmen. The capitalist does not hire workers for charity but for profit. Having "freely" entered into a contract with the capitalist, the worker must labour on, producing extra value and beyond that sum agreed on as his wage.

The means of production on the one hand, and labour power on the other—the "factors of production" of bourgeois economics—represent the different forms assumed by the original capital in the second phase of the cycle:

MONEY - COMMODITY - MONEY

(purchase) (production) (sale)

Capitalist economists treat these factors as equal. Marxism distinguishes between that part of capital which does not undergo any change of value in the process of production (machines, tools, raw materials) and that part represented by labour power which creates new value. The first part of capital called constant capital, and the latter variable capital. The total value of a commodity is made up from constant capital, variable capital and surplus value, i.e.

C + V + S.

Necessary and Surplus Labour

The labour performed by the working class can be divided up into two parts:

(1) Necessary Labour: This is the part of the labour process which is needed to cover the cost of wages.

(2) Surplus Labour: This is the extra labour performed in addition to labour, which produces the profits.

To increase his profits, the capitalist is constantly attempting to reduce his wages bill. He does this by attempting to (1) lengthen the working day, introduce new shift patterns, etc., (2) increase productivity to cover wages more quickly, (3) resist wage rises or attempt to cut them.

Rate of Surplus Value

Since the whole purpose of capitalist production is to extract surplus value from the labour of the working class, the proportion between variable capital (wages) and the surplus value (profits) is of the greatest importance. One is expanding or contracting at the expense of the other. This struggle over the surplus constitutes the class struggle. What concerns the capitalist is not so much the amount of surplus value produced but the rate of surplus value. For every pound he lays out in capital he expects a big return. The rate of surplus value is the rate of exploitation of labour by capital. It may be defined as S/V or surplus labour/necessary labour, (it is the same thing expressed in a different way), where V = Variable capital, S = Surplus value. For example in a small plant, total capital of £500 is divided between Constant (£410) and Variable (£90). Through the process of production the value of the commodities have increased by £90 surplus: (C+V) + S or (410 + £90) + £90 surplus. The total new value is £590.

It is the variable capital that is the living labour, i.e. it produces the new value of surplus value. So the relative increase in the value produced by variable capital gives us the rate of surplus value S/V = £90/£90 =100% rate of surplus value.

The Rate of Profit

Under the pressure of competition at home and abroad, the capitalist is compelled to constantly revolutionise the means of production and to increase productivity. The need to expand compels him to spend a larger and larger proportion of his capital on machinery and raw materials and less on labour power, thus diminishing the proportion of variable capital to constant capital. Side by side with automation goes the concentration of capital, the liquidation of the smaller concerns and the domination of the economy by giant monopolies. This constitutes a change in the technical composition of capital.

But since it is the variable capital (labour power) alone which is the source of surplus value (profit), the bigger amounts invested in constant capital results in the tendency for the rate of profit to fall, although with new investments profits can increase enormously, they do not rise proportionately to the much greater capital outlay.

For example, take a small capitalist with a total capital of £150 made up of Constant Capital (£50) and Variable (£100). He employs 10 men at £10 per day making tables and chairs. After one day work they produce £250 in total value:

Total Capital:

The wages paid = £100

The constant capital = £50

Surplus value = £100

The rate of surplus value can be calculated: S/V = £100/£100 = 100%. The rate of profit is calculated as the ratio between total capital and surplus value: Surplus Value/Total capital or £100/£150 = 66.66 % rate of profit. As the amount of constant capital is increased, so the rate of profit falls. In the same example given the same rate of surplus value we increase the constant capital from £50 to £100. The rate of profit = Surplus value/Total capital = £100/£200 = 50%. Again if we increase the constant capital to £200, all other things being equal, Surplus Value/Total Capital = £100/£300 = 33.33 % rate of profit. And lastly constant capital is increased to £300, the rate of profit would be £100/£400 = 25%.

This increase in constant capital expresses in Marxist terms a higher organic composition of capital, and is a progressive development of the productive forces. The tendency is therefore built into the very nature of the capitalist mode of production, and has been one of the major problems facing the capitalist class in the post-war period. The mass of surplus value increases, but in proportion to the increased size of constant capital it results in a falling rate of profit. The capitalists have continually attempted to overcome this contradiction by the increased exploitation of the working class, to increase the mass of surplus value and therefore the rate of profit, by means other than investment. They do this in a number of ways by raising the intensity of exploitation, increasing the speed of the machinery and the lengthening of the working day. Another method to restore the rate of profit is to cut the real wages of the workers below their real value. The very laws of capitalism gives rise to enormous contradictions. The capitalists' constant striving for profits gives the impetus for investment, but new technology forces more workers on the scrap heap. Yet paradoxically the only source of profit is from the labour of the working class.

Export of Capital

The highest stage of capitalism—imperialism—is marked by the enormous export of capital. In their search for increased rates of profit, the capitalists are forced to invest huge sums of money abroad in countries of low composition of capital. Eventually, the whole world, as Marx and Engels explain in the *Communist Manifesto* becomes dominated by the capitalist mode of production.

One of the major contradictions of capitalism is the obvious problem that the working class as consumers have to buy back what they have produced. But as they do not receive the full value of their labour, they have not the resources to do this. The capitalists solve this contradiction by taking the surplus and reinvesting it in developing the productive forces further. Also they seek to sell the remaining surplus on the world market in competition with the capitalists of all the other different countries. But there are also limits to this as all the capitalists of the world are playing the same game. In addition, the capitalists resort to credit, via the banking system, to provide the necessary cash for the mass of the population to buy the goods. But this also has its limits as the credit eventually has to be paid back, with interest.

That explains why periodically, the booms are followed in regular succession by periods of slump. The feverish struggle for markets end up in a crisis of overproduction for capitalism. The destructiveness of the crisis, which are met with the wholesale writing-off of accumulated capital, are a sufficient indication of the impasse of capitalist society.

All the factors that led to the world upswing after the war have prepared the way for downswing and crisis. The characteristic of this new epoch is the organic crisis that capitalism now faces. At some stage the working class will be faced with a 1929-type slump if capitalism is not eradicated. Only by overthrowing the anarchy of capitalist production can humanity prevent the chaos, wastage and barbarism of capitalism. Only by eliminating private property of the means of production, can society escape the laws of motion of capitalism and develop and blossom in a planned and rational way. The mighty forces of production, built by class society, can abolish once and for all the criminal scandal of so-called overproduction in a world of want and starvation. Eradicating the contradiction of the development of the productive forces and the nation state and private ownership, will provide the basis for an international plan of production.

Using the powers of science and technology, the whole of the planet could be transformed in the space of a decade. The socialist transformation of society remains the most urgent and burning task facing the world's working class. Marxism provides the weapon and understanding to weld together this mighty army for the establishment of a socialist Britain, a socialist Europe, and the basis for the World Federation of Socialist States.

Glossary

The following glossary compiles brief definitions of the central terms employed by Marx in Volume I of *Capital*. Many of these terms are used in various senses and with diverse shades of meaning. We hope, therefore, that the reader will both find this glossary useful and be aware of its limitations.

absolute surplus-value: surplus-value produced by extending the length of the working day beyond necessary labour time and thus directly augmenting surplus labour time.

abstract labour: labour in its general or quantitative aspect as a producer of value, abstracted from its particular qualities as labour productive of a certain kind of use-values.

capital: value capable of self-expansion through the purchase and use of labour-power (a social relation) and the consequent production of surplus-value.

capital accumulation: the reinvestment (or capitalisation) of a portion of surplus-value in new elements of constant and variable capital, thereby increasing the scale of production; also termed 'extended reproduction' and 'concentration of capital.'

centralisation of capital: combination of individual capitals to form larger capitals. as in mergers and takeovers.

collective labourer: a cooperative combination of workers, e.g., made necessary by capitalism's socialization of the labour process; under capitalism, the collective labourer includes all those agents who perform productive labour for capital including intellectual workers in the sphere of production.

commodity: a product of human labour which is produced in order to be exchanged.

composition of capital: the division of capital into that part which purchases material means of production (constant capital) and that part which purchases labour-power (variable capital); in terms of use-values: the 'technical composition of capital'; in value terms: the 'value composition of capital, the term 'organic composition of capital' expresses the dependence of the value composition on the technical composition.

concrete labour: labour as work of particular kind; labour as a creator of use-values; labour in its qualitative aspect.

constant capital: that part of capital which purchases material means of production (raw materials, auxiliary materials, and instruments of labour); that part of advanced capital which does not expand its value in production.

exchange-value: the relative proportions in which commodities exchange for each other on the market; an expression of their value or the form in which value is manifested.

fetishism of commodities: the mistaken idea that the value of a commodity is an intrinsic property of the commodity as an object; the failure to understand how exchange relations are determined by social relations.

forces of production: include the technical division of labour, the means of production, and the knowledge and skills available to the producers; the forces of production combine with the relations of production to provide the basis for a mode of production.

intensity of labour: the degree of effort expended in work; labour more intense than average creates more use-values, and hence more value than average in a given time.

labour-power: literally, the capacity for work; the commodity the labourer sells to the capitalist in exchange for wages; the use-value of labour-power is labour; its value is the value of the commodities comprising the worker's subsistence.

labour process: the process of creating use-values; its factors include the activity of the worker, the instruments of labour, and the subject of labour.

manufacture: that mode of production based upon a detailed division of handicraft labour within the workplace; entails the 'formal subjection' (social subordination) of labour to capital without fundamentally altering the technical basis of production.

means of production: the material factors of the labour process, including raw materials, auxiliary materials, and instruments of labour.

mode of production: literally, 'a way of producing,' used by Marx in several senses; the strongest sense is the one that combines forces and relations of production; each mode of production (e.g., the capitalist mode of production) represents a combination of a fundamental class relation, labour process, and form of extraction of surplus labour.

modern industry: that mode of production, specific to capitalism, which affects not only the social organization of production, but revolutionizes as well, its technical basis and, in so doing, results in the 'real subjection' of labour to capital.

money: a commodity (typically, gold or other precious metal) which serves as a universal value equivalent and consequently as the measure of value and the medium of commodity circulation.

necessary labour: that part of the working day during which the labourer produces value equal to the value of his labour-power, value that he realizes in his wage.

price: the expression of value in money; sometimes the actual exchange proportions of commodities which may depart from their values (e.g., because of supply and demand).

primitive accumulation: the historical process of separating the independent commodity producer from the means of production; this separation ensures the existence of wage labour and therefore is a fundamental condition of capitalist production; additionally, all accumulation from outside the capitalist mode of production may be seen as primitive accumulation.

productive labour: under capitalism, labour which produces surplus-value for capital.

productivity (productiveness): the quantity of use-values of a particular sort produced in a certain amount of labour time; thus the value of commodities varies inversely with the average social productivity of the labour which creates them.

relations of production: the class relations necessitated by a particular mode of production; every mode of production combines forces and social relations of production; in the capitalist mode of production, the fundamental relation of production is the wage relation between the capitalist class and the working class.

relative surplus population: working-class population in excess of the needs of capital; serves to regulate wages through the supply of and demand for labour.

relative surplus-value: surplus-value produced as a consequence of shortening necessary labour time, for example, by decreasing the value of subsistence goods

revenue: that portion of surplus-value which the capitalist spends for his personal consumption.